lazy days
and beach blankets

lazy days

and beach blankets

Simple alfresco dining with family and friends

RYLAND
PETERS
& SMALL

LONDON NEW YORK

First published in the United States in 2009
by Ryland Peters & Small, Inc.
519 Broadway, 5th Floor
New York, NY 10012
www.rylandpeters.com

10 9 8 7 6 5 4 3 2 1

Text © Ghillie Basan, Fiona Beckett, Susannah
Blake, Maxine Clark, Ross Dobson, Clare Ferguson,
Liz Franklin, Tonia George, Brian Glover, Jane
Noraika, Louise Pickford, Ben Reed, Fiona Smith,
Sunil Vijayakar, Fran Warde, Lindy Wildsmith,
and Ryland Peters & Small 2009

Design and photographs
© Ryland Peters & Small 2009

Library of Congress Cataloging-in-Publication Data
Lazy days and beach blankets: simple alfresco
dining with family and friends. -- 1st ed.
      p. cm.
   Includes index.
   ISBN 978-1-84597-845-7
   1. Cookery, International. 2. Outdoor cookery.
   TX725.A1L324 2009
   641.9--dc22   2008050367

Printed and bound in China.

Notes

• All spoon measurements are level, unless
otherwise stated.

• Eggs are medium unless otherwise specified.
Uncooked or partially cooked eggs should not
be served to the very old, frail, young children,
pregnant women, or those with compromised
immune systems.

• To sterilize preserving jars, wash them in hot,
soapy water and rinse in boiling water. Place in
a large pan and cover with hot water. With the
lid on, bring the water to a boil and boil for
15 minutes. Turn off the heat and leave the jars
in the hot water until just before they are to be
filled. Invert the jars onto paper towels and let
dry. Sterilize the lids for 5 minutes, by boiling, or
follow the manufacturer's instructions. Jars should
be filled and sealed while still hot.

Design Toni Kay and Paul Tilby
Editor Helen Ridge
Picture Research Emily Westlake
Production Toby Marshall
Art Director Leslie Harrington
Publishing Director Alison Starling

Indexer Hilary Bird

contents

Parasols and picnic rugs

Lazy days outside are meant to be hassle-free and all about enjoying good company, simple food, and thirst-quenching drinks. This book is designed to give you plenty of inspiration for meals, snacks, cocktails, and summery settings to help you make the most of glorious sun-filled afternoons and long, balmy evenings. Here are a few helpful tips if you are planning to eat alfresco with family and friends:

• Depending on the number of guests you are expecting, you will need extra chairs and a large table, plus flatware, cutlery, and glasses. All these things can be hired if you need to.

• Choosing what to cook is the fun part—try to offer a balance of meat, poultry, fish, and seafood plus vegetables and some vegetarian alternatives.

• Plan well ahead so you can order ingredients in advance. Shop for the non-perishables a week ahead and then many of the raw ingredients can be bought the day before and others picked up early on the day of the party.

• If you are having a cook-out, always check that you have plenty of fuel for the barbecue (unless you have a mains gas or electric grill). Keep a spare full gas bottle or buy double the amount of charcoal you need—you can always use it next time.

• Order drinks in advance and don't forget to ask for "sale or return"—over-order rather than under-order. The same supplier may be used to hire glasses. Order plenty of non-alcoholic drinks as well, for non-drinkers, designated drivers, and children.

• Food and drink must be kept cold, so make as much room in the refrigerator as you can for the food—line up the cool boxes for salads, and hire garbage cans or plastic tubs for drinks and fill them up with ice. Have the drinks delivered cold, and pack them in ice as soon as they arrive.

• Evening parties need plenty of tea lights, storm lanterns, and large candles to add a lovely ambience to the evening.

• Burning citronella candles and mosquito coils will help to keep the bugs at bay.

• If you are cooking on an outside grill, find a sheltered spot with little or no wind to blow smoke and sparks, but close enough to the kitchen for convenience. Choose a flat non-flammable surface, such as a terrace or flat grassy area. Avoid cooking on a wooden deck as sparks or embers may drop through.

• To ensure that what we eat is safe for us we must take the steps necessary to avoid food poisoning which, although rarely life-threatening, can be extremely unpleasant. Young children, the elderly, and pregnant women are particularly vulnerable to illness caused by unsafe foods, and the main way that food becomes contaminated is by poor storage or dirty utensils. It's important to always keep foods covered with plastic wrap while they are waiting to be cooked.

• All cooked foods are safest eaten soon after cooking and most grilled foods cooked on a barbecue are best eaten hot from the fire. If you are grilling vegetables to eat later, then cool them as quickly as possible and chill in the refrigerator until required.

• Remember health issues when cooking pork and poultry—always make sure the meat is cooked through before eating. This can be done either by using an instant-read thermometer or by inserting a skewer into the thickest part of the meat. If the juices run clear, the meat is cooked. If they are still bloody, return to the stove, broiler, or grill and continue cooking.

snacks & sides

This is a fun version of garlic bread, and the slightly smoky flavor from the coals is delicious. You can also add cubes of cheese such as mozzarella or fontina to the skewers.

garlic bread skewers

1 baguette

2/3 cup extra virgin olive oil

2 garlic cloves, crushed

2 tablespoons chopped fresh parsley

sea salt and freshly ground black pepper

6–8 wooden skewers, soaked in water for 30 minutes

Serves 6–8

Preheat the grill.

Cut the bread into 1-inch slices, then cut the slices crosswise to make half moons.

Put the olive oil, garlic, parsley, salt and pepper into a large bowl, add the bread, and toss until well coated with the parsley and oil.

Thread the garlic bread onto skewers and cook over medium-hot coals for 2–3 minutes on each side until toasted.

Variation Cut 8 oz. mozzarella cheese into about 24 small pieces. Thread a piece of bread onto the skewer and continue to alternate the cheese and bread. Cook as in the main recipe.

green olive and basil paste

This unusual Provençal-style paste is delicious, especially when spread on crisp crackers and served with a glass of something chilled. It's also very easy to make.

8 oz. green olives stuffed with anchovies in brine or 8 oz. pitted green olives in brine and 4 canned anchovy fillets

2 garlic cloves, chopped

half a handful of fresh basil leaves, torn into pieces

1 slice stale bread, wetted and squeezed dry

1/4 cup extra virgin olive oil

1–2 teaspoons white wine vinegar (optional)

salted crackers, tiny oven-dried ficelle toasts, small crispbreads or baby romaine lettuce leaves, to serve

Serves 4–6

Put all the ingredients except the oil and vinegar into a food processor. Whizz for 30 seconds.

With the machine running, drizzle in enough olive oil to create a pleasant texture.

Taste, add vinegar to season, if liked, then do a final burst of processing to combine.

Serve with salted crackers, tiny oven-dried ficelle toasts, or small crispbreads. Baby cos lettuce leaves are another option.

Variation Substitute the chopped leaves from 8 stems of fresh French tarragon for the basil.

dried tomato purée

Made from sun-dried and kiln-dried tomatoes, this paste has an intense, sweet-sharp taste, enlivening soups and sauces, as well as adding new interest to the appetizer tray.

3 1/2 oz. sun-dried or kiln-dried tomatoes

2 tablespoons extra virgin olive oil

4 garlic cloves, peeled

1 teaspoon coarse sea salt

1/2 teaspoon dried oregano or rosemary, crumbled

1 teaspoon fennel or anise seeds

5 tablespoons boiling water or vegetable stock

1/4 cup dry white wine

crudités, young salad leaves, toasts, or hard-cooked egg halves, to serve

Serves 4

Scissor-snip the tomatoes into small pieces. Heat the olive oil in a skillet and add the tomatoes.

Pound together the garlic, salt, oregano, and fennel seeds using a pestle and mortar. Add to the tomatoes and stir over high heat until aromatic. Pour in the boiling liquid and cook over medium heat, stirring, for a further minute, until most of the liquid has evaporated. Turn off the heat. Add the wine, then cover and let sit for 5 minutes.

Tip the skillet contents into a food processor and whizz until the mixture becomes a rough paste, about 15–20 seconds. Let cool.

Spoon the paste into one or more serving dishes. Smooth the surface and chill.

Serve with crudités, young salad leaves, toasts, or hard-cooked egg halves.

Black, glossy tapenade gets its name from *tapeña*, the Provençal word for "caper." This essential ingredient, along with salted anchovies, canned tuna (optional), garlic, herbs, olive oil, *marc (eau de vie)*, or lemon juice or both, creates a heady mix. Use tapenade on toast, and eat with hard-cooked egg halves and raw carrot, celery, fennel, cucumber, and tomato. It also makes a good sauce for poached fish or steaks. These days, green olives, sweet bell peppers, and sun-dried tomatoes often go into so-called tapenades, but black olives create the true classic.

tapenade

12 oz. dry-cured, soft black olives (to yield 8 oz. pitted olives)

1/2 cup salted capers, rinsed

6 fresh salted anchovies, boned, rinsed, and chopped, or 12 canned anchovy fillets, chopped

2 oz. canned tuna in brine, drained and flaked

2–4 garlic cloves, crushed

1 teaspoon mixed dried herbs, including thyme, oregano, lavender, and savory

1/2 teaspoon coarse sea salt

freshly ground black pepper

4–6 tablespoons extra virgin olive oil

1 tablespoon marc de Provence (eau de vie)

freshly squeezed juice of 1/4 lemon (optional)

garlicky toasts and arugula leaves, to serve

Serves 4–6

Pit the olives and put in a food processor with the capers, anchovies, and tuna. Process, in bursts, to a pulp.

Put the garlic, herbs, salt, and pepper into a large mortar, and pound with a pestle to create a pungent paste. Gradually work in the olive pulp, then process in bursts, with the oil, until creamy.

Taste and add the marc and the lemon juice, if liked, for balance.

Drizzle the mixture over garlicky toasts and top with arugula leaves. Alternatively, serve with grilled fish or roast lamb, or mixed into butter for grilled steaks.

Eggplants of all sizes, colors, and shapes are the glory of market stalls throughout Provence; every cook can afford this ingredient. The joky title of this recipe implies (justifiably) that eggplants are precious in their own right. Local cooks roast them in the oven or over charcoal but they can also be grilled directly over gas flames, spiked between two forks.

beggar's caviar

2 medium eggplants (about 1 lb. in total)

2 garlic cloves, crushed

3 canned salted anchovy fillets

1/4 cup extra virgin olive oil

sea salt and freshly ground black pepper

torn fresh basil or scissor-snipped lovage or flatleaf parsley (optional), to garnish

crusty bread or small toasts, to serve

Serves 4–6

Preheat the broiler and position an oven rack about 3 inches below the heat source.

Pierce each eggplant six times or so with a fork, then place on the rack. Cook for 10 minutes. Turn over and cook for a further 10 minutes. Alternatively, push forks into both ends of each eggplant, turn the gas burner to its highest and flame-grill each one, turning at intervals so that they are evenly charred, hot, and cooked through, about 6 minutes each. Let cool.

Peel off most of the eggplant skin and discard the leafy stem ends. Drain off any juice.

Put the garlic, anchovies, salt, and pepper in a mortar and pound together with a pestle. Add about a quarter of an eggplant and continue to pound.

Transfer the mixture and all the remaining eggplant flesh to a food processor. Pulse briefly in half-a-dozen 5-second bursts, drizzling in the olive oil at intervals. This will create an earthy-textured paste.

Taste and season again. Spoon into a serving dish, sprinkle with your preferred fresh herb, then serve warm or cool, with crusty bread or small toasts.

Hot from the grill, this aromatic herb bread is delicious eaten on its own with olive oil for dipping.

grilled rosemary flatbread

1²/₃ cups bread flour, plus extra for dusting

1¹/₂ teaspoons active dry yeast

1 teaspoon salt

1 tablespoon chopped fresh rosemary

¹/₂ cup hot water

2 tablespoons extra virgin olive oil, plus extra for brushing

Serves 4

Preheat the grill to low.

Sift the flour into the bowl of an electric mixer and stir in the yeast, salt, and rosemary. Add the hot water and olive oil and knead with the dough hook at high speed for about 8 minutes or until the dough is smooth and elastic. Alternatively, sift the flour into a large bowl and stir in the yeast, salt, and rosemary. Make a well in the center, then add the hot water and olive oil and mix to form a soft dough. Turn out onto a lightly floured work surface and knead until the dough is smooth and elastic.

Shape the dough into a ball, then put into an oiled bowl, cover with a dish towel, and let rise in a warm place for 45–60 minutes or until doubled in size.

Punch down the dough and divide into 4. Roll each piece out on a lightly floured work surface to make a 6-inch long oval.

Brush the bread with a little olive oil and barbecue for 5 minutes, then brush the top with the remaining olive oil, flip, and barbecue for a further 4–5 minutes until the bread is cooked through.

Serve hot with olive oil for dipping.

sun-dried tomato, olive, and basil bread

1½ cups all-purpose flour

1 tablespoon baking powder

3 extra large eggs

6 tablespoons milk

6 tablespoons olive oil

3½ oz. Gruyère cheese, grated

3½ oz. sun-dried tomatoes in oil, drained and roughly chopped

2 oz. pitted black olives marinated with herbs, roughly chopped

a small handful of basil leaves, roughly sliced

sea salt and freshly ground black pepper

a 12 x 4-inch nonstick loaf pan, lightly greased and floured

Serves 6

These easy breads are very popular in France where they are somewhat confusingly called "cake." They're like a cross between a savory bread and a quiche, and delicious to nibble with drinks.

Preheat the oven to 350°F.

Sift the flour with the baking powder and season well with salt and black pepper. Beat the eggs and beat in the milk and oil. Tip two-thirds of the liquid into the flour, beat well, then add the remaining liquid. Mix in the Gruyère, tomatoes, olives, and basil, then tip into the prepared loaf pan. Bake in the preheated oven for 50 minutes or until a skewer comes out clean. Let cool, then remove from the pan. Wrap in aluminum foil and keep in the refrigerator.

Serve at room temperature, sliced and cut into halves or squares. You could also serve a plate of some chunky handcut, slices of salami that can be eaten with your fingers.

toasted ciabatta pizzas

Other breads can be used in these fantastic, fresh-tasting pizzas, so don't go shopping specially for ciabatta. You can also use Jack or blue cheese instead of mozzarella.

1 loaf ciabatta, split lengthwise or sliced

1 garlic clove, peeled

about ¼ cup olive oil

4 ripe tomatoes, peeled and sliced

a handful of pitted olives

a bunch of marjoram

10 oz. mozzarella cheese

a bunch of basil

sea salt and freshly ground black pepper

Serves 4

Preheat the oven to 350°F.

Broil the ciabatta under a hot broiler until lightly toasted, then rub with the garlic, using it like a grater. Put the garlic ciabatta on a baking sheet and drizzle with a little of the olive oil.

Arrange the sliced tomatoes on the bread, then add the olives, marjoram, mozzarella, basil, salt, and pepper. Drizzle more oil over the top.

Cook in the preheated oven for 15–20 minutes until the tomatoes are softened and crisp around the edges and the mozzarella has melted.

three salsas

Salsas give an extra dimension to chicken, meat, and fish and are incredibly versatile. The hot pineapple and papaya salsa is good with shrimp or pork, the creamy corn salsa marries well with chicken, while the tomato and ginger salsa is very good with white fish or tortilla chips.

creamy corn salsa

1 ear of fresh corn, husk removed

2 red chiles

1 tomato, diced

1 garlic clove, crushed

freshly squeezed juice of 1/2 lime

1 tablespoon maple syrup

2 tablespoons sour cream

sea salt and freshly ground black pepper

Serves 6

Preheat the grill until hot.

Add the corn and cook for about 15 minutes, turning frequently, until charred on all sides. Let cool.

Add the chiles and cook until the skins are charred all over. Transfer to a bowl and cover with a clean cloth until cool.

Using a sharp knife, cut down all sides of the corn cob to remove the kernels. Put them into a bowl. Peel and seed the chiles, chop the flesh, and add it to the corn.

Stir in all the remaining ingredients, season to taste, then serve.

hot pineapple and papaya salsa

1/2 ripe pineapple

1/2 large papaya

freshly squeezed juice of 1 lime

1–2 green chiles, seeded and finely chopped

2 scallions, finely chopped

1 tablespoon chopped fresh mint

1 tablespoon Thai fish sauce

Serves 6

Peel the pineapple, remove and discard the core, then dice the flesh and put into a serving bowl, together with any juice.

Peel the papaya, scoop out the seeds, and dice the flesh. Add to the pineapple.

Stir in the scallions, mint, and fish sauce, set aside to infuse for about 30 minutes, then serve.

tomato, sesame, and ginger salsa

2 ripe tomatoes, peeled, seeded, and diced

1/2 red onion, finely chopped

2 inches fresh ginger, peeled and grated

1 garlic clove, chopped

1 tablespoon chopped fresh cilantro

2 tablespoons peanut oil

1 tablespoon soy sauce

1 teaspoon sesame oil

Serves 6

Put all the ingredients into a bowl, set aside to infuse for about 30 minutes, then serve.

2 cups dried peeled fava beans

1 fresh bouquet garni of parsley, celery, bay leaf, and thyme

1 large onion, chopped

1 potato, unpeeled

4 garlic cloves, chopped

1/4 cup extra virgin olive oil, plus extra to serve (optional)

freshly squeezed juice of 1 lemon

6 sprigs of fresh oregano, chopped

sea salt and freshly ground black pepper

your choice of baby leafy vegetables, radishes, crusty bread, cucumber, to serve

Serves 4

All round the Mediterranean, fresh and dried peas, beans, and lentils are used in dips and spreads, as sauces with pasta, and in soups. Depending on the region and local herbs, different flavors and ingredients are used. Near Nice, Swiss chard stems and parsley may be added; in Italy, rosemary is used rather than oregano; and in North African immigrant communities, mint may be an option. The constant is dried fava beans. The best are the skinless type: they cook quickly, taste better, and have a more delicate texture. Soak them for 4 hours or overnight in cold water, or cheat by putting them in a saucepan, covering them with boiling water, bringing to a boil, and soaking for 2 hours with the heat turned off. Drain, cover with cold water, bring to a boil, and simmer until tender. Drain again, season, and use as a dip or spread (or dilute as a sauce or soup).

italian bean dip

Soak and drain the beans as described above, then put them in a large saucepan with the bunch of herbs, onion, and potato and add 2 quarts boiling water. Bring to a boil, boil hard for 10 minutes, reduce the heat, and cook, partially covered, for 1½–2 hours or until you can crush the beans easily with your thumbnail.

Drain the vegetables and discard the herbs. Working in batches if necessary, put the beans, potato, onion, and garlic in a food processor, with the olive oil, lemon juice, oregano, salt, and pepper. Blend in short bursts to a grainy but creamy purée.

Serve hot (as a side dish), warm, or cool, sprinkled with extra olive oil. Serve as a dip or spread with baby leafy vegetables, radishes, and cucumber or with bread chunks, or a combination.

8 oz. for each serving of fresh, young, summer vegetables, washed and trimmed, such as baby carrots, baby fennel bulbs, radishes, cherry tomatoes, baby zucchini

Bagna cauda

4 tablespoons unsalted butter

3–4 large garlic cloves, crushed

2 oz. canned anchovies in oil, drained and chopped

¾ cup extra virgin olive oil

Serves 4–6

summer vegetables
with bagna cauda

Put the bagna cauda—the "hot bath"—of warm anchovy butter in the center of the table with a basket of fresh summer vegetables, so everyone can just help themselves.

Arrange the trimmed vegetables in a basket or on a large platter.

To make the bagna cauda, put the butter and garlic into a small saucepan and heat gently. Simmer very slowly for 4–5 minutes until the garlic has softened, but not browned. Add the anchovies, stir well, then pour in the oil. Cook gently for a further 10 minutes, stirring occasionally, until the sauce is soft and almost creamy.

Transfer the sauce to a dish and serve at once with the selection of trimmed vegetables.

18 small artichokes

1 lemon, halved

2 tablespoons extra virgin olive oil

sea salt and freshly ground black pepper

lime wedges, to serve

Chile lime mayonnaise

1 dried chipotle chile

2 egg yolks

1¼ cups olive oil

freshly squeezed juice of 1 lime

sea salt

Serves 6

Small or baby artichokes are best for this dish because they can be barbecued without any blanching first.

grilled artichokes with chile lime mayonnaise

To make the mayonnaise, cover the dried chile with boiling water and let soak for 30 minutes. Drain and pat dry, then cut in half and scrape out the seeds. Finely chop the flesh and put into a food processor. Add the egg yolks and a little salt and blend briefly until frothy. With the blade running, drizzle the oil through the funnel until the sauce is thick and glossy. Add the lime juice

and, if the mayonnaise is too thick, a tablespoon of warm water. Taste and adjust the seasoning, then cover and set aside.

Preheat the grill.

Trim the stalks from the artichokes and cut off the top 1 inch of the globes. Slice the globes in half lengthwise, cutting out the central "choke," if necessary. Rub the cut surfaces all over with lemon juice to stop them discoloring.

Toss the artichokes with the oil and a little salt and pepper. Barbecue over medium-hot coals for 15–20 minutes, depending on size, until charred and tender, turning halfway through the cooking time. Serve with the mayonnaise and wedges of lime.

Gooey, caramelized garlic spread over lightly grilled toast is the perfect outdoor appetizer for keeping your guests happy while you're finalizing the lunch preparations.

bruschetta with caramelized garlic

1 whole head of garlic

a sprig of fresh thyme

1 tablespoon extra virgin olive oil, plus extra to sprinkle

4 slices sourdough or ciabatta bread

sea salt and freshly ground black pepper

Serves 4

Preheat the grill.

Cut the top off the garlic head to reveal the cloves. Put the head onto a piece of foil, add the thyme sprig, and season with salt and pepper. Sprinkle with the olive oil, then fold over the foil, sealing the edges to form a parcel. Cook over hot coals for about 20 minutes or until the garlic is softened.

Put the bread slices on the grill rack and toast for a few minutes on each side. Squeeze the cooked garlic out of the cloves and spread onto the toasted bread. Sprinkle with a little more olive oil, season with salt and pepper, and serve while still warm.

Variation Try topping the garlic with slices of Camembert cheese and sprinkle with extra virgin olive oil.

cilantro flatbreads
with spiced eggplants and split pea dip

Give yourself plenty of time to make the bread, and try to time the last batch of baking so that the aromas leave your guests in no doubt that the bread is homemade. Serve with a salad of tomato, red onion, and herbs.

Preheat the oven to 400°F.

To make the flatbreads, put the flour in a large bowl, then stir in the yeast, salt, cumin seeds, cilantro, and chile. Make a well in the center and add the water. Mix with your hands to form a dough. Either transfer to an electric mixer fitted with a dough hook or continue kneading by hand for about 10 minutes or until the dough is smooth and springy to the touch. Return to the bowl, lightly brush the top with oil, then cover with plastic wrap. Let rise in a warm place for 30–40 minutes.

To make the spiced eggplants, put the lemon juice, chile, mint, olive oil, salt, and pepper in a blender and process until smooth. Put the eggplants and red onions on the baking sheet. Pour the olive oil mixture over the vegetables and massage in well with your hands. Bake in the preheated oven for 30 minutes, then transfer to a serving bowl and top with the parsley. Turn up the oven temperature to 450°F.

To make the dip, put the yellow split peas in a medium saucepan, then cover with cold water and add the salt. Bring to a boil and cook for 30–40 minutes until soft. Drain, then transfer to a food processor. Add the cumin, lemon juice, garlic, and olive oil and blend to a smooth purée. Add salt and pepper to taste, then transfer to a bowl and sprinkle with extra olive oil and some dill.

Meanwhile, to cook the flatbreads, transfer the dough to a lightly floured work surface and knead for a few minutes. Divide into 20–25 balls. Using a rolling pin, roll the dough balls into thin, flat ovals. Put on a lightly greased baking sheet and cook in batches in the preheated oven for 15–20 minutes until golden and puffy. Serve with the spiced eggplants and split pea dip and a salad of tomato, red onion, and herbs.

Cilantro flatbreads

5 cups white bread flour, plus extra for dusting

1/4 oz. package active dry yeast

2 teaspoons sea salt

1 tablespoon cumin seeds, lightly toasted in a dry skillet

a large handful of fresh cilantro, chopped

1 red chile, seeded and finely chopped

about 4 cups warm water

olive oil, for brushing

Spiced eggplants

freshly squeezed juice of 1 lemon

1 red chile, seeded and chopped

a large handful of fresh mint leaves, finely chopped

1/2 cup olive oil

3 eggplants, cut into chunks

1 red onion, cut into wedges

fresh flatleaf parsley, chopped, to serve

sea salt and freshly ground black pepper

Split pea dip

2 cups yellow split peas

1 teaspoon sea salt

1 teaspoon cumin seeds, lightly toasted in a dry skillet, then ground in a coffee grinder

freshly squeezed juice of 1 lemon

2 garlic cloves, crushed

1/4 cup olive oil, plus extra to serve

fresh dill, coarsely chopped, to serve

sea salt and freshly ground black pepper

1–2 large baking sheets, lightly greased

Serves 4

Topping

2 tablespoons olive oil

2 large sweet onions (about 1 lb. in total), thinly sliced

1 garlic clove, finely chopped

1 teaspoon finely chopped thyme or 1/2 teaspoon dried thyme

5 oz. small pitted marinated black olives

sea salt and freshly ground black pepper

a few small basil leaves, to garnish

Pastry dough

3 1/2 oz. Quark or cream cheese

7 tablespoons unsalted butter, cut into cubes, at room temperature

1 cup all-purpose flour

1 teaspoon baking powder

a good pinch of salt

a 3-inch pastry cutter

2 x 12-cup shallow tartlet pans

Makes about 12–14

mini pissaladières

These tartlets make a sophisticated and popular addition to any picnic. They can also be made in advance, frozen, and then reheated from frozen in a moderate oven, which all helps to take the pressure off you on the day.

Heat the oil in a large flameproof casserole or saucepan. Tip in the onions, then cook over medium heat until they have begun to collapse (about 10 minutes). Stir in the garlic and thyme, turn the heat down a little, and continue to cook for another 30–40 minutes until the onions are soft and golden and any liquid has evaporated, taking care that they don't catch and burn. Season with salt and pepper and set aside to cool.

While the onions are cooking, make the pastry dough. Tip the Quark into a food processor with the softened butter and process until smooth. Sift the flour with the baking powder and salt and add to the creamed cheese and butter in 2 batches, using the pulse to incorporate it. Once the mixture starts to form a ball, turn it out of the processor onto a floured board and form it into a flat disc. Put it in a plastic bag and chill for an hour in the refrigerator.

When ready to make the tartlets, preheat the oven to 425°F. Roll out the pastry dough quite thinly. Stamp rounds out of the dough, re-rolling the trimmings as necessary, and lay them in the hollows of the tartlet pans. Spoon in teaspoonfuls of the cooled onion mixture and top with an olive. Bake for 15–20 minutes until the dough is puffed up and golden.

Cool for 10 minutes, then remove the tarts carefully from the pan and arrange on a plate. Scatter with a few small basil leaves and serve.

turkish toasted bread

Indian and Middle Eastern stores stock a wide variety of unusual and delicious items, including a range of different breads that can be used for this recipe.

Preheat the oven to 325°F.

Put the harissa, cilantro, olive oil, olives, and chiles in a small bowl and mix well. Divide the mixture between the pieces of bread, then sandwich the halves back together.

Put on a baking sheet and cook in the preheated oven for 10 minutes. Remove and serve hot.

* Harissa paste is a hot blend of chiles and spices available from Middle Eastern markets, gourmet stores, and some supermarkets. It's great to have on hand for firing up all sorts of dishes. Stir it into couscous or mix with yogurt and serve as a dip for crudités.

1 teaspoon harissa paste*

a bunch of fresh cilantro, chopped

2 tablespoons olive oil

1/4 cup pitted olives, chopped

2 red chiles, seeded and chopped

4 slices small Turkish flatbread, pita bread, or small flour tortillas, separated into disks

a baking sheet

Serves 4

stuffed focaccia bread

This superb focaccia really does not take too long to prepare, and the aroma is totally beguiling.

3¹/₃ cups white bread flour

¼ oz. package active dry yeast

1 tablespoon olive oil, plus extra to brush

sea salt

small sprigs of fresh rosemary

Filling

½ red bell pepper, halved, seeded, and sliced

½ orange bell pepper, halved, seeded, and sliced

1 red onion, sliced

olive oil, for roasting

8 oz. mozzarella cheese, cut into cubes

a large handful of fresh basil, chopped

8 sun-dried tomatoes in oil, sliced, plus 1 tablespoon of the oil

a handful of pitted black olives

sea salt and freshly ground black pepper

a baking sheet, lightly greased and floured

Serves 6–8

Preheat the oven to 350°F.

To make the dough, put the flour, 1 teaspoon salt, and the yeast in a large bowl. Stir in the oil and 1½ cups water, then bring the dough together with your hands. Knead the dough by hand until it is smooth and springy to the touch (this should take about 10 minutes) or knead in a machine with a dough hook attachment. Return to the bowl and lightly oil the top to prevent it from drying out. Cover with plastic wrap or a damp dish towel and let rise in a warm place for 30 minutes until doubled in size.

Meanwhile, to prepare the filling, put the bell peppers and onion in a roasting pan, sprinkle with olive oil and salt, and roast in the preheated oven for 15 minutes. Remove from the oven and let cool. Transfer to a bowl, add the mozzarella, basil, tomatoes, oil, olives, salt, and pepper, and mix well.

When the dough has risen to double its original size, transfer to a lightly floured surface and cut in half. Roll out the first half to the size of the baking sheet and use to line the tray. Spread the filling over the top, leaving a 1-inch border around the edge. Roll out the remaining dough and put on top of the filling. Press the edges of the dough together to seal.

Brush with the 2 teaspoons olive oil, sprinkle with salt, and dot with sprigs of rosemary, then let rise for a further 30 minutes. Just before cooking, use your thumb to make lots of indentations in the dough—this looks very attractive when cooked. Bake in the preheated oven for 40 minutes until lightly golden.

Chicken Caesar salad has traveled all over the world, and many additions to the basic lettuce and croûtons with cheese and anchovy dressing can be found. This variation, wrapped in a tortilla, is a great idea for a picnic dish.

chicken caesar wrap

Broil or sauté the bacon for 2–3 minutes until crisp. Cool, then cut into thin strips. Roughly shred the chicken into large strips.

To make the dressing, put the egg yolk into a small bowl, add the lemon juice, Worcestershire sauce, and a little salt and pepper and beat until frothy. Gradually beat in the oil, a little at a time, until thickened and glossy. Add 2 tablespoons water to thin the sauce, then stir in the cheese.

Lay the tortilla flat on a work surface and arrange a little lettuce down the middle of each one. Top with chicken, bacon, anchovies, a spoonful of the dressing and, finally, more lettuce. Wrap the tortilla into a roll, then wrap the roll in a napkin. Repeat to make 6 wraps. Serve immediately or chill to serve later.

3 large strips of bacon

8 oz. cooked chicken breast

6 small flour tortillas

1 large romaine lettuce, shredded (inner leaves only)

12 anchovy filiets in oil, drained and chopped

Caesar dressing

1 egg yolk

1 tablespoon freshly squeezed lemon juice

1 teaspoon Worcestershire sauce

1/2 cup olive oil

1/4 cup freshly grated Parmesan cheese

sea salt and freshly ground black pepper

Serves 6

2 red bell peppers, left whole

4 small focaccia or Turkish rolls, halved

2 large, cooked chicken breasts, shredded

a small handful of baby spinach

Arugula aïoli

1 egg yolk

1 teaspoon white wine vinegar

a bunch of arugula, about 2 oz., coarsely chopped

1 garlic clove, crushed

2/3 cup olive oil

sea salt and freshly ground black pepper

Serves 4

Panini, which is Italian for toasted sandwiches, can be prepared ahead of time, then cooked just before you want to serve them. The combination of grilled peppers, tender chicken, and a delicious arugula aïoli is definitely hard to beat.

chicken panini
with roasted bell pepper and arugula aïoli

Preheat the grill, then cook the bell peppers over hot coals or under a preheated broiler for about 20 minutes until charred all over. Put into a plastic bag and let cool. Peel off the skin and discard the seeds, then cut the flesh into strips.

To make the aïoli, put the egg yolk, vinegar, and a little salt and pepper into a food processor and blend briefly until frothy. Add the arugula and garlic and pulse for 30 seconds. With the machine still running, gradually pour in the olive oil until the sauce is thickened and speckled with vivid green. Taste and adjust the seasoning.

Spread a little of the arugula aïoli onto the cut sides of each roll and fill the rolls with the chicken, pepper strips, and spinach leaves. Press the halves together.

Preheat the flat plate on the grill and cook the panini over low heat for 4–5 minutes, then, using tongs, flip over and cook the other side for a further 5 minutes until toasted. If you don't have a flat plate, cook on a cast-iron griddle, either on the grill, or on the stove. Serve hot.

In Sicily, this is known as *cabbucio*, meaning hood or cowl, and refers to a kind of bruschetta with a lid. Authentic Italian bread is still additive-free, which means it goes stale quickly, but put yesterday's uncut loaf in a hot oven for a few minutes and it will come out like new. Cut it open while hot and anoint it with extra virgin oil and your chosen filling and you have a delicious snack. Alternatively, you can use fresh bread.

hot crusty loaf filled with mozzarella, salami, and tomato

1 lb. round "flat" crusty Italian loaf

5 large tomatoes, thinly sliced

6 1/2 oz. mozzarella cheese, thinly sliced

3 1/2 oz. sliced salami or prosciutto, or whole anchovy fillets

a small bunch of oregano or basil

sea salt and freshly ground black pepper

extra virgin olive oil, for drizzling

Serves 4

Preheat the oven to 425°F.

Heat the bread in the preheated oven for 5 minutes. While the bread is still hot, cut it in half lengthwise and make small incisions all over the cut surfaces of both halves of the bread. Drizzle with olive oil and sprinkle with salt, pepper, and half the oregano leaves. On the bottom half of the loaf, put a layer of tomato, followed by a layer of cheese. Top with the salami and the remaining oregano leaves. Sandwich the 2 halves together, wrap in aluminum foil and a clean dish towel, then transfer to a picnic basket.

Spain's celebrated thick tortilla omelet (*tortilla de patata*) is one of the world's most accommodating dishes. It's good for any occasion, particularly as a portable picnic food, but it's also very useful as a quick lunch dish eaten between slices of bread and even as a breakfast snack. Served with this scarlet sweet pepper sauce, it is delicious. In many Spanish bars and cafés, sliced zucchini, spinach, onion, or red bell peppers may be added to the potatoes for variety, flavor, and color, but plain potato is the most common and well loved at home and abroad.

spanish potato omelet

1/2 cup extra virgin olive oil

2 lb. boiling potatoes, peeled and cut into 1-inch cubes

1 onion, sliced into rings

4 garlic cloves, finely chopped (optional)

6 eggs, beaten

1/4 cup chopped fresh flatleaf parsley or scallion tops

sea salt and freshly ground black pepper

Sweet pepper sauce

8 oz. can or jar of roasted sweet peppers, such as piquillos or pimientos

3 tablespoons sherry vinegar

Serves 4–6

Heat the oil in a medium skillet, add the potatoes and onion, and cook over low heat for 12–14 minutes or until tender but not browned, moving them about with a spatula so that they cook evenly. Add the garlic, if using, for the last 2 minutes.

Put the eggs, salt, and pepper in a bowl and beat well.

Using a slotted spoon, remove the cooked potatoes and garlic from the pan and stir it into the egg mixture. Stir in the parsley.

Quickly pour the egg mixture back into the hot skillet. Cook, not stirring, over low to moderate heat for 4–5 minutes or until firm, but do not let it brown too much. The top will still be wobbly and only partially cooked.

Holding a heatproof plate over the top of the omelet, quickly invert the pan, omelet, and plate. Slide the hot omelet back, upside down, to brown the other side for 2–3 minutes more, then remove from the pan and let cool for 5 minutes.

To make the sauce, put the sweet peppers, 1/3 cup of the liquid from the can (make it up with water if necessary) and the sherry vinegar in a blender. Purée to form a smooth, scarlet sauce.

Cut the omelet into chunks, segments, or cubes. Serve the sauce separately, spooning some over the pieces of tortilla.

With its lovely, earthy flavors, a frittata is an Italian version of the Spanish tortilla or the French omelet, and different ingredients are added depending on the region or season. Eaten cold, it is ideal for a picnic.

mixed mushroom frittata

3 tablespoons extra virgin olive oil

2 shallots, finely chopped

2 garlic cloves, finely chopped

1 tablespoon chopped fresh thyme leaves

3 cups mixed wild and cultivated mushrooms, such as chanterelle, portobello, shiitake, and white button mushrooms

6 eggs

2 tablespoons chopped fresh flatleaf parsley

sea salt and freshly ground black pepper

Serves 6

Put 2 tablespoons of the oil into a nonstick skillet, heat gently, then add the shallots, garlic, and thyme. Sauté gently for 5 minutes until softened but not browned.

Meanwhile, brush off any dirt clinging to the mushrooms and wipe the caps. Chop or slice coarsely and add to the skillet. Sauté for 4–5 minutes until they just start to release their juices. Remove from the heat.

Put the eggs into a bowl with the parsley and a little salt and pepper, beat briefly, then stir in the mushroom mixture. Wipe the skillet clean. Preheat the broiler.

Heat the remaining tablespoon of oil in the clean skillet and pour in the egg and mushroom mixture. Cook over medium heat for 8–10 minutes until set on the bottom. Transfer to the preheated broiler and cook for about 2–3 minutes until the top is set and spotted brown. Cool at room temperature before taking outdoors.

chilled avocado and bell pepper soup

A cold soup on a hot summer's day is difficult to beat. The secret is to make it look gorgeous while keeping the portions small. Glasses are a great idea for serving, showing off the vibrant green color—utterly seductive.

1 tablespoon olive oil

1/2 onion, finely chopped

1 green bell pepper, seeded and finely chopped

1/2 green chile, seeded and finely chopped

6 cups vegetable stock

freshly squeezed juice of 1 lime

1 avocado, halved and pitted

a handful of fresh mint leaves

sea salt and freshly ground black pepper

Greek yogurt, to serve

crushed ice, to serve

Serves 4

Put the oil, onion, bell pepper, and chile in a saucepan and cook over gentle heat for about 20 minutes until completely soft. Let cool.

Transfer to a blender, add the vegetable stock, lime juice, avocado flesh, and mint leaves, and purée until smooth. Add salt and pepper to taste, then serve in bowls or glasses, topped with a spoonful of yogurt and some crushed ice.

This combination of salad leaves, all of them refreshing in taste and intense in color, makes a cracking chilled summer soup. Plunging lightly cooked leaves and vegetables into ice water helps preserve their natural green pigment.

chilled spinach, arugula, and watercress soup

4 shallots, chopped

2 garlic cloves, chopped

1/2 nutmeg, grated, plus extra to serve

1/3 cup white wine

1 3/4 cups vegetable stock

8 oz. mixed spinach, arugula, and watercress leaves

3/4 cup light cream or yogurt

sea salt and freshly ground black pepper

olive oil, for sautéing

4 teaspoons light cream, to serve

4 large leaves of arugula, to serve

Serves 4

Heat enough olive oil to cover the base of a skillet, add the shallots, garlic, and nutmeg and sauté over low heat until the onions are soft. Add the wine and stock and bring to a boil, then simmer for 10 minutes. Remove from the heat and let cool.

Put the spinach, arugula, and watercress in a large pan containing 1 quart of lightly salted boiling water, gently submerse the leaves with a spoon, and blanch for 60 seconds. Drain and plunge the leaves into a bowl of cold water and ice to chill quickly. Drain and squeeze out the excess water with your hands.

Put the leaves and the soup in a food processor and blend to a smooth consistency. Add the cream and season with salt and pepper to taste. Cover and chill for at least 2 hours or overnight.

Ladle the soup into bowls, feather with cream, and serve with arugula leaves and grated nutmeg.

Gazpacho is the famous iced tomato soup from Andalucia. This recipe calls for sweetly mellow Pedro Ximenez vinegar, produced from one of Spain's most distinguished sweet wines and available from good wine merchants, but if you can't find it, use sherry vinegar and sweet sherry instead. Serve the chilled soup with olive ice cubes in stemmed glasses on a small plate, as seen in tapas bars from Seville to Salvador. The flavor of the tomatoes is important. Green bell peppers, always included in Andalucia, are not everyone's favorite, so omit them if you prefer.

gazpacho pedro ximenez

To make decorative ice cubes, start the day before. Set 12 stuffed olives in an ice-cube tray. Fill it with sparkling water and freeze. Keep until serving time.

Put the tomatoes, onion, cucumber, pepper, if using, and the tomato paste in a food processor or blender. Add the garlic, stale bread, half the vinegar, all the oil, and 1¾ cups water. Purée the soup continuously until it becomes

a smooth, brick-red mixture. Add salt and pepper to taste, then add the remaining vinegar. Blend again.

Pour into 4–6 stemmed glasses, each with 2–3 olive ice cubes. Set the remaining olives on the plate. Drink the soup straight from the glass: the olives act as additional seasoning.

Variations If you prefer, omit the olive-filled ice cubes and simply serve plain ice, with extra olives on the side.

To make croûtons, cut an additional 1–1½ slices of stale bread into ½-inch cubes and sauté in extra virgin olive oil until crisp. Serve with the soup for sprinkling on top.

2 vine-ripened tomatoes, blanched, peeled, and finely chopped

½ red or white onion, finely chopped

1 cucumber, peeled and finely chopped

1 green bell pepper, seeded and chopped (optional)

1 tablespoon tomato paste

2 garlic cloves, chopped

1 cup stale bread cubes, about 1 slice

3 tablespoons Pedro Ximenez vinegar, or sherry vinegar plus 1 tablespoon sweet sherry

1 tablespoon extra virgin olive oil

sea salt and freshly ground black pepper

Green olive ice cubes

12 green Spanish olives, stuffed with anchovies or almonds

chilled sparkling water

Serves 4–6

salads

sweet glazed bell pepper salad

Don't think that there are too many bell peppers in this recipe—they will definitely all disappear!

10 red bell peppers, cut into large chunks and seeded

5 red onions, quartered lengthwise

1/4 cup olive oil

1/3 cup balsamic vinegar

2 tablespoons clear honey

12 oz. pitted kalamata or other black olives, chopped, about 2 1/2 cups

sea salt and freshly ground black pepper

a sprig of parsley, to serve

Serves 20

Preheat the oven to 350°F.

Put the bell peppers and onions into a large bowl, add the olive oil, and mix to coat. Transfer to 2 large roasting pans and cook in the preheated oven for 1 hour, turning the vegetables after 40 minutes so they will cook evenly. Add the vinegar, honey, olives, salt, and pepper, mix well, and set aside to cool.

Serve warm or cold, topped with a sprig of parsley.

summer salad

This quick and simple salad sparkles with the good, clean, peppery taste of watercress and the delicious crunch of radish and celery.

10 oz. watercress, ends trimmed

a bunch of radishes, trimmed and halved, about 10

6 celery ribs, sliced

1/4 cup olive oil

2 tablespoons balsamic vinegar

sea salt and freshly ground black pepper

Serves 4

Put the watercress in a salad bowl, then add the halved radishes and sliced celery.

Drizzle with the olive oil. Add the vinegar and seasoning, toss well, and enjoy.

Cook's tip Some salad items are not good travelers and by the time they make it from your shopping basket to the table, they may have seen better days. Replace any of the ingredients in the above salad with whatever is fresh and best in the market on the day.

Pumpkin seeds and pumpkin seed oil seem to be back in fashion. Look for dark, sticky, roasted pumpkin seed oil in gourmet stores, and use it quickly because it won't keep well after opening. Alternatively, keep in the coolest, darkest part of the refrigerator.

red leaf salad

2 small heads of radicchio (round shaped)

2 heads pointed red Belgian endive

2 heads Italian-style pointed red escarole

1/4–1/2 head of red oakleaf lettuce

2 handfuls baby red chard leaves

1 tablespoon extra virgin olive oil

1/4 cup husked pumpkin seeds

1 red onion, cut into fine segments or rings

Dressing

3 tablespoons extra virgin olive oil

1/4 cup roasted pumpkin seed oil or extra virgin olive oil

1 tablespoon red wine or sherry vinegar

2 teaspoons Dijon mustard

1 tablespoon crème de cassis (optional)

sea salt and freshly ground black pepper

Serves 4

Wash the radicchio, endive, escarole, lettuce, and chard and separate into leaves. Dry well.

Put the 1 tablespoon olive oil in a skillet, add the pumpkin seeds, and toss over low heat until toasted and aromatic (take care because they can burn easily). Remove from the heat and let cool on a plate.

To make the dressing, put the olive and pumpkin seed oils in a salad bowl, add the vinegar, mustard, crème de cassis, if using, salt, and pepper and beat with a fork until emulsified.

Add the leaves, red onion, and pumpkin seeds, toss well, then serve.

This satisfying summer salad with a delicious hint of fresh mint makes a superb accompaniment to barbecued meat or fish.

zucchini, feta, and mint salad

Preheat the grill.

Put the sesame seeds into a dry skillet and toast over medium heat until golden and aromatic. Remove from the heat, let cool, and set aside until required.

Cut the zucchini diagonally into thick slices, toss with the olive oil, and season with salt and pepper. Cook over hot coals for 2–3 minutes on each side until charred and tender. Remove and let cool.

Put all the dressing ingredients into a screw-top jar and shake well. Add salt and pepper to taste. Put the zucchini, feta, and mint into a large bowl, add the dressing, and toss well until evenly coated. Sprinkle with the sesame seeds and serve at once.

1 tablespoon sesame seeds

6 medium zucchini

3 tablespoons extra virgin olive oil

6 oz. feta cheese, crumbled

a handful of fresh mint leaves

Dressing

1/4 cup extra virgin olive oil

1 tablespoon freshly squeezed lemon juice

1 small garlic clove, crushed

sea salt and freshly ground black pepper

Serves 4

bean and mint salad

This mix of beans and fresh mint is very refreshing and clean on the palate, making it a great summer salad.

8 oz. fava beans, shelled and peeled

3/4 cup green peas, shelled

3 oz. dwarf or French beans, trimmed

3 oz. runner beans, sliced into 2-inch pieces

8 scallions, trimmed and sliced

a large bunch of fresh mint, coarsely chopped

3 tablespoons olive oil

grated zest and freshly squeezed juice of 1 unwaxed lemon

sea salt and freshly ground black pepper

Serves 4

Cook the fava beans in a large saucepan of boiling water for 4 minutes, then add the peas, dwarf or French beans, and runner beans and continue cooking for 3 minutes. Drain, cool quickly under cold running water, then drain thoroughly.

Put the scallions and mint in a large bowl. Add the beans, then sprinkle with the olive oil, lemon zest and juice, salt, and pepper. Toss well and serve.

Cook's tip Turn this salad into an entrée by adding crumbled feta cheese, sliced hard-cooked eggs, or pieces of juicy roasted ham.

leaf and herb salad

This may be a simple salad, but simplicity is best when you're working with the fragrant flavors of herbs. To make it extra pretty, garnish with edible flowers such as heartsease, nasturtiums, and pansies, when available.

10 oz. mixed leaves or 1 head of lettuce

a handful of edible flowers (optional)

4 bunches of herbs, such as basil, chives, marjoram, flatleaf parsley, sage, tarragon, fennel, and lovage

extra virgin olive oil, to drizzle

Serves 4

Wash and trim the mixed leaves or lettuce as necessary. Tear into a bowl. Add the edible flowers, if using, and a selection of your chosen herbs. Drizzle with olive oil, toss well, and serve immediately.

For this Arab-influenced salad, try to use young, tender fennel bulbs and vividly juicy and colorful oranges (or try it with minneolas, clementines, satsumas, or mandarins.) To cut off all of the bitter pith, slice a piece off the top and base of each fruit, then slice off the skin and white pith from top to bottom using a fine, serrated vegetable knife, in a sawing movement—easy and effective. Orange flower water is sold in Italian and Middle Eastern shops.

fennel and orange salad

5 large oranges, about 1¹/₂ lbs., or equivalent weight of minneolas, clementines, satsumas, or mandarins, washed and dried

1–2 heads of young fennel, preferably with green tops

2 red onions, thinly sliced

24 black olives, preferably the dry-cured Provençal type

Dressing

¹/₄ cup extra virgin olive oil

¹/₂ teaspoon orange flower water or 1 tablespoon freshly squeezed orange juice

1 teaspoon sea salt

¹/₂ teaspoon white, green, or pink peppercorns, well crushed or chopped

Serves 4

Using a vegetable peeler, remove the zest of 1 orange or 2 smaller citrus fruits, then slice the zest into thin strips. Set aside. Halve and squeeze the juice from the zested fruit into a bowl.

Remove a slice from the top and bottom of the remaining fruit, then prepare as described in the recipe introduction. Discard the debris. Slice each fruit crosswise into thin rounds, adding any juice to the bowl.

Finely slice the fennel bulb lengthwise. Toss it immediately in the bowl of juice. Assemble the fennel, oranges, onions, and olives on a flat salad platter, then add the reserved zest and pour the juice over the top.

To make the dressing, put the olive oil, orange flower water, salt, and pepper in a bowl or jar and beat or shake well. Pour the dressing over the salad and serve cool.

salade niçoise

2 garlic cloves, lightly crushed and halved

1 head of romaine lettuce, or 1/2 head of Batavia or frisée

1 small Boston lettuce or other crisp baby lettuce (optional)

2 scallions, sliced

8–12 oz. good-quality canned tuna pieces or cooked, cold, fresh tuna

2 oz. salted anchovies or 24 canned salted anchovy fillets

24 black olives, Niçoise type (optional)

3 or 4 hard-cooked eggs, peeled and quartered or halved

a handful of fresh, small basil leaves, roughly torn

6 1/2 oz. fresh fava beans, shelled and peeled

2 ripe red tomatoes, each cut into 6 or 8 wedges

4-inch piece of cucumber, peeled and cubed

2 fresh baby artichokes, trimmed, halved, and chokes removed (or canned equivalent)

4 radishes, sliced

1/2 cup extra virgin olive oil

1/2 teaspoon sea salt

1 lemon, cut into wedges (optional)

Serves 4–6

This is probably one of the world's best-known (but least well-made) salads. Debate rages over its provenance, but certain facts about its content seem immutable: anchovy fillets and canned, good-quality tuna are vital, as are hard-cooked eggs. Also essential are tomatoes, cucumber, green bell pepper, onion, raw fava beans, and basil leaves, while tender baby artichokes, ideally raw, are desirable. Black olives are optional, but usual. No cooked vegetables whatsoever are allowed, but if fava beans are unavailable, break the rules and substitute 5 oz. briefly cooked thin green beans. The garlic is best rubbed around the bowl, but it can also be crushed into the olive oil and lemon dressing poured over the salad. (However, many maintain that lemon is not permissible.) Think of this salad as a celebration of fresh flavors.

Rub the garlic cloves around the base and sides of each salad plate or bowl.

Wash and shake dry the salad leaves, then cover and chill. Tear them and use some of each type to line the plates or bowls. Scatter in some scallions.

Break the tuna into coarse chunks and place on the lettuce. Rinse and dry the anchovies if very salty, then arrange in a criss-cross pattern on the tuna. Add the olives (if using), eggs, and basil. Dot with the fava beans, tomatoes, cucumber, artichokes, and radishes.

Whisk together the oil and the salt, adding the juice from 1 lemon wedge (if using). Drizzle this dressing over the salad just before serving, and put a wedge of lemon on each plate, if liked.

Pan bagnat

This dish, literally "bathed bread" (from tomato juices and dressing), is essentially salade Niçoise packed into a large round *boule* or country loaf, the middle of which has been scooped out. It can also be made with lengths of hollowed-out baguette. The bread is pressed flat, wrapped in waxed paper, tied up, and a weight placed on top. In 2–3 hours it is ready to unwrap and eat.

Cut pan bagnat looks gloriously colorful, like a layered terrine, and makes a splendid picnic dish.

kisir

This Turkish recipe is the perfect party salad. You can vary it depending on what you have available, substituting walnuts for hazelnuts or pistachios, for example, adding some olives or some finely snipped dried apricots or replacing the dill with fresh cilantro.

1½ cups bulgur wheat

¼ cup roasted hazelnuts, chopped

¼ cup pistachio nuts, chopped

5–6 scallions, trimmed and thinly sliced

½ cucumber, peeled, seeded, and finely chopped

1 red bell pepper, halved, seeded, and finely chopped

3 ripe tomatoes, peeled and finely chopped

1 pomegranate

freshly squeezed juice of 2 lemons

½ teaspoon sea salt

1 teaspoon ground cumin

1 teaspoon red pepper flakes

3 tablespoons extra virgin olive oil

1 tablespoon pomegranate syrup or 2 teaspoons balsamic vinegar with 1 teaspoon sugar

5 tablespoons finely chopped fresh flatleaf parsley

3 tablespoons finely chopped fresh mint leaves

3 tablespoons finely chopped fresh dill

sea salt and freshly ground black pepper

Serves 8

Put the bulgur wheat in a large heatproof bowl and pour over enough boiling water to just cover the grain. Leave for 15 minutes for the liquid to absorb, then pour over plenty of cold water, swirl the grain around, and tip into a sieve. Squeeze the grain with your hands to extract any excess water and return the grain to the bowl.

Add the nuts, scallions, cucumber, bell pepper, and tomatoes (including the seeds and pulp). Halve the pomegranate and scoop out the seeds, reserving the juice and discarding the pith. Add the pomegranate seeds to the salad.

Whisk the lemon juice and reserved pomegranate juice with the salt, cumin, and red pepper flakes, whisk in the olive oil and pomegranate syrup and season with salt and pepper. Tip into the salad and mix well.

Finally, mix in the chopped herbs. Toss well together and check the seasoning, adding more salt, pepper, or lemon juice to taste. Cover and set aside for at least an hour before serving for the flavors to infuse.

This dish, cooked on top of the stove, produces almost confit-style tomatoes; the more usual way is to oven-bake them. However, this homely method is very easy, especially for households without an oven, and luscious too.

Provençal tomatoes

6 medium ripe, flavorful tomatoes, halved horizontally

1 teaspoon sea salt

1 teaspoon sugar

8 black peppercorns

¼ nutmeg, freshly grated

2 shallots, finely chopped

2 tablespoons extra virgin olive oil

2 garlic cloves, crushed or chopped

a handful of chopped mixed fresh herbs, such as chives, parsley, tarragon, borage, oregano, and sage, or 2 teaspoons Provençal mixed dried herbs (if no fresh available)

3–4 tablespoons water, stock, or white wine

3 tablespoons bread crumbs, pan-sizzled in 1 tablespoon extra virgin olive oil

Serves 4

Scoop out and discard the seeds and juice from the tomatoes (or reserve for use another time).

Using a pestle and mortar, grind together the salt, sugar, and peppercorns. Stir in the nutmeg. Sprinkle the tomatoes with this mixture, and put some shallots inside each one.

Heat the olive oil in a large, wide, heavy-based skillet over high heat for 2 minutes. Add the tomatoes in a single layer, hollow side up. Scatter in the garlic and half the herbs, then cook for 2 minutes on a fairly high heat, uncovered.

Add 2 tablespoons of the water, stock, or wine. Cover the skillet, reduce the heat to its lowest setting, and cook for 10 minutes more.

Use a spoon and palette knife to turn the tomatoes, being careful to keep neat shapes. If there is no liquid left, add 2 more tablespoons of the water, stock, or wine. Cover the skillet again and continue cooking for 10 minutes more. By now the tomatoes should be sticky, nearly collapsed, and very fragrant.

Serve them right side up, with any of the sticky reside from the skillet, and sprinkled with the remaining fresh herbs and a few toasted bread crumbs, if liked. Enjoy hot, warm, or cool.

camargue rice salad

Inspired by the cuisine of Camargue in southern Provence, this rice salad is excellent served warm, cool, or cold.

3¹/₂ tablespoons salted butter

2 red onions, sliced

1 cup Camargue red rice, washed and drained

¹/₂ cup Camargue or other long-grain white rice, washed and drained

1 fresh bouquet garni of thyme, sage, bay, and oregano

2 dried chiles, crushed but whole

finely grated zest and freshly squeezed juice of 1 orange

finely grated zest and freshly squeezed juice of 1 unwaxed lemon

1¹/₂ teaspoons sea salt

¹/₃ cup capers

¹/₃ cup green or black olives

2 tablespoons concentrated chicken bouillon or
1 stock cube, crumbled

Serves 4–6

Heat a heavy-based flameproof casserole and melt the butter. Sauté the red onions over high heat for 2 minutes.

In a separate pan, bring 1⅔ cups of water to a boil, add the red rice and return to a boil. Reduce the heat to a simmer, cover the pan, and cook for 25–30 minutes, or until the rice is al dente.

Scatter the white rice and all the remaining ingredients (reserving a little zest) into the pan with the onions. Add ¾ cup boiling water.

Return to a boil, then simmer, covered, for 10–12 minutes, or until the rice is tender and all the liquid has been absorbed. Remove the bouquet garni and chiles. Stir in the cooked red rice.

To serve, pile up the rice, scatter with the reserved citrus zests, and eat as a warm salad. Alternatively, serve cool or cold.

fava bean salad with mint and parmesan

This salad, served with a hazelnut oil dressing, makes a wonderful addition to a picnic spread. If it's early in the season and you have young, tender fava beans, it's not necessary to peel them after blanching. Out of season, you can use frozen fava beans or flat beans cut into 1-inch lengths.

1–1½ lbs. shelled, young fresh or frozen fava beans

3 Belgian endives

leaves from 3 sprigs of fresh mint

1 oz. Parmesan cheese

Dressing

2 tablespoons extra virgin olive oil

¼ cup hazelnut oil*

2 teaspoons white wine vinegar

1 teaspoon Dijon mustard

¼ teaspoon sugar

sea salt and freshly ground black pepper

Serves 6

Plunge the fava beans into a saucepan of lightly salted, boiling water, return to a boil, and simmer for 1–2 minutes. Drain and refresh the beans immediately under cold running water. Pat dry and gently peel away the gray-green outer skin if necessary. Put the peeled beans into a salad bowl.

Cut the endives in half lengthwise, slice thickly crosswise, then add to the beans. Add the mint leaves, tearing any large ones in half. Using a potato peeler, cut thin shavings of Parmesan over the salad.

Just before serving, put the dressing ingredients into a small pitcher, mix well, sprinkle over the salad, toss well, then serve.

* If hazelnut oil is difficult to find, substitute extra virgin olive oil. Always buy nut oils in small quantities and keep them in the refrigerator: they are delicate, and become rancid very quickly.

Fresh mozzarella is essential for this recipe. Made from cow's or buffalo's milk, these soft white balls of cheese are best enjoyed within a day or two of being made. This fresh cheese is quite different from the firmer yellow mozzarella frequently used on pizza and lasagne.

mozzarella, peach, and frisée salad

3 fresh peaches, cut into thin wedges

4 handfuls of frisée leaves, trimmed

1 large ball of buffalo mozzarella, torn into thin shreds

3 tablespoons extra virgin olive oil

1 tablespoon white wine vinegar

freshly ground black pepper

Serves 4

Put the peach wedges and frisée in a large bowl and gently toss to mix. Arrange on a serving plate. Scatter the mozzarella pieces over the salad.

Put the olive oil, vinegar, and black pepper in a bowl, whisk with a fork, and then spoon over the salad to serve.

Variations Replace the mozzarella with 5 oz. crumbled firm blue cheese and the frisée with spinach leaves. Alternatively, keep the mozzarella and replace the other ingredients with fresh slices of tomato, basil leaves, and some fruity extra virgin olive oil.

Orzo is a rice-shaped pasta, ideal for making into a salad because it retains its shape and texture after cooking.

orzo salad
with lemon and herb dressing

8 oz. cherry tomatoes, halved

1/3 cup extra virgin olive oil

8 oz. orzo or other tiny soup pasta*

6 scallions, finely chopped

1/4 cup coarsely chopped mixed fresh herbs, such as basil, dill, mint, and parsley

grated zest and freshly squeezed juice of 2 unwaxed lemons

sea salt and freshly ground black pepper

4 wooden skewers, soaked in water for 30 minutes

Serves 4

Preheat the grill or broiler.

Thread the tomatoes onto the soaked wooden skewers with all the cut halves facing the same way. Sprinkle with a little olive oil, season with salt and pepper, and grill or broil for 1–2 minutes on each side until lightly charred and softened. Remove from the heat and set aside.

Bring a large saucepan of lightly salted water to a boil. Add the orzo and cook for about 9 minutes or until al dente. Drain well and transfer to a large bowl.

Heat 2 tablespoons of the olive oil in a skillet, add the onions, herbs, and lemon zest, and stir-fry for 30 seconds. Stir into the orzo, then add the tomatoes, lemon juice, remaining olive oil, salt, and pepper. Toss well and let cool before serving.

* If orzo is unavailable, use other pasta shapes, such as ditalini or pennetti, instead.

pasta, squash, and feta salad
with olive dressing

Tapenade is an essential ingredient of the olive dressing. You can buy this paste ready-made but by far the best tapenade is the one you make yourself (page 12).

1 1/2 lbs. butternut squash

1 tablespoon extra virgin olive oil

1 tablespoon chopped fresh thyme leaves

1 lb. dried penne

10 oz. feta cheese, diced

10 oz. cherry tomatoes, about 2 cups, halved

1/4 cup chopped fresh basil

1/4 cup pumpkin seeds, pan-toasted in a dry skillet

sea salt and freshly ground black pepper

Dressing

1/2 cup extra virgin olive oil

3 tablespoons Tapenade (page 12)

freshly squeezed juice of 1 lemon

1 teaspoon clear honey

sea salt and freshly ground black pepper

Serves 6

Preheat the oven to 400°F.

Peel and seed the butternut squash and cut the flesh into bite-size pieces. Put into a bowl or plastic bag, then add the oil, thyme, salt, and pepper, Toss well, then arrange in a single layer in a roasting pan. Roast in the preheated oven for about 25 minutes until golden and tender. Let cool.

To make the dressing, put the olive oil, tapenade, lemon juice, and honey into a bowl. Whisk well, then add salt and pepper to taste.

Bring a large saucepan of lightly salted water to a boil, add the penne, and cook for about 10 minutes until al dente. Drain well, then stir in 1/4 cup of the dressing. Let cool.

When cool, put the pasta and squash into a salad bowl, mix gently, then add the feta cheese, cherry tomatoes, basil, and toasted pumpkin seeds. Just before serving, stir in the remaining dressing.

lobster salad
with chile dressing

Ready-cooked and halved lobsters are easy to find, and some people may prefer to buy them like this rather than prepare them from scratch. But, if you have time and want to cook them yourself, it's well worth it because you can guarantee that the lobster will be really fresh. If lobsters are difficult to get, or too expensive, try substituting monkfish, often called "poor man's lobster," or even boneless chicken breasts, tossed in olive oil, then roasted in a hot oven for about 25 minutes. Seed the chiles in the dressing only if you are fearful of heat.

8 small or 4 large lobsters

1¹/2 lbs. potatoes, cut into chunks

a bunch of fresh cilantro, coarsely chopped

1 red onion, very thinly sliced

sea salt and freshly ground black pepper

leafy salad greens, to serve

Dressing

1 green or red chile, seeded (optional) and chopped

2 inches fresh ginger, peeled and chopped

5 garlic cloves, crushed

2 tablespoons white wine vinegar

¹/3 cup sugar

Serves 8

To make the dressing, put the chile, ginger, and garlic into a saucepan. Add the vinegar and sugar and simmer over low heat, stirring frequently, for 10 minutes, until reduced by half. Add 2 tablespoons water, remove from the heat, and let cool.

If cooking the lobsters live, bring a large saucepan of water to a boil. Plunge the lobsters carefully into the boiling water, cover with a lid, and simmer for 10 minutes per pound. Drain and let cool.

When cool, remove the claws and legs. Using a large, sharp knife, split each body in half lengthwise, holding the lobster with a dish towel in your other hand to stop it slipping. Crack open the claws and remove the flesh, leaving it in whole pieces. Remove the flesh from the split body halves and cut into thick slices. Reserve the shells.

Cook the potatoes in a saucepan of boiling, salted water for 20 minutes, until tender when pierced with a knife. Drain and let cool. Add the cilantro and chopped lobster to the potatoes, with salt and pepper to taste. Mix lightly, then spoon the mixture into the empty lobster shells, piling it in generously. Spoon over the dressing, sprinkle with the onion slices, and serve with leafy salad greens.

If you've never eaten a Japanese salad, this will be a delightful surprise. The salad itself is a simple combination of fresh ingredients plus two types of Japanese noodles—but it's the dressing that makes this so interesting.

japanese garden salad
with noodles

4 oz. soba noodles

4 oz. udon noodles

8 oz. snowpeas, about 1¹/2 cups

2 romaine lettuce hearts, leaves separated

2 carrots

1 cucumber

4 ripe tomatoes

Dressing

2 tablespoons Japanese soy sauce (shoyu)

1¹/2 tablespoons sugar

1¹/2 tablespoons rice vinegar

1 tablespoon sesame oil

Serves 6

Cook the noodles separately according to the instructions on the packages. Drain and set aside.

Blanch the snowpeas in lightly salted, boiling water for 1 minute. Drain, refresh under cold water, and dry well.

Wash and dry the lettuce leaves. Cut the carrot and cucumber into matchsticks and the tomatoes into wedges. Divide the noodles and salad ingredients between 6 serving bowls.

Put the dressing ingredients into a bowl, add ¹/2 cup water, and stir well until the sugar has dissolved. Pour over the salad and serve at once.

Asparagus in season is pure delight. Add the delicate sweetness of prosciutto, dried to crispness, and you have an unusual combination. Use white asparagus if you can find it (French and Italian grocers often stock this during early summer), though green asparagus is more usual. This dish goes particularly well served with *frizzante*, such as Lambrusco, or a crisp, dry, white wine.

asparagus with prosciutto

8 thin slices prosciutto

1 lb. bunch of thick asparagus

2 tablespoons extra virgin olive oil or lemon oil

Serves 4

Before turning on the oven, hang the slices of prosciutto over the grids of the top oven rack. Slide the rack into the oven, then turn it on to 300°F. Leave for 20 minutes until the prosciutto has dried and become crisp. Remove it carefully and set aside.

Preheat the broiler. Using a vegetable peeler, peel 3 inches of the tough skin off the end of each asparagus spear, then snap off and discard any tough ends. Arrange the asparagus on a shallow baking sheet and sprinkle with the oil. Cook under the preheated broiler for 6–8 minutes, or until the asparagus is wrinkled and tender.

Serve the asparagus with some of the hot oil from the broiler pan and 2 prosciutto "crisps" for each person.

ham and melon platter

For color contrast you need an orange Canteloupe or Charentais melon and a green Galia, Ogen, or Honeydew melon, and some thinly sliced prosciutto. Quarter and seed the melons, cut the wedges off the skin, then cut them into thick slices. Arrange on a big plate along with loosely draped slices of ham. The platter wants to look quite casual—lavish and generous, rather than arranged into perfectly lined up rows.

Serve the platter with some olive breadsticks and mini ciabattas, refreshed in the oven.

chicken salad
with radicchio and pine nuts

This salad is delightful, with the rich, almost plum-like flavors of its Marsala raisin dressing. If you can't find sherry vinegar, one of the most delicious vinegars, use balsamic instead.

1 small red onion, sliced

1¹/2 lbs. cooked chicken breast

1 head of radicchio, shredded

4 oz. arugula leaves

a few sprigs of flatleaf parsley

Dressing

¹/3 cup extra virgin olive oil

¹/2 cup pine nuts

¹/2 cup raisins

2 tablespoons Marsala wine

2 tablespoons sherry vinegar

sea salt and freshly ground black pepper

Serves 4–6

Put the onion slices into a small bowl and cover with cold water. Let soak for 30 minutes, drain well, then dry thoroughly with paper towels.

Tear or slice the chicken into thin strips and put into a large salad bowl. Add the radicchio, arugula leaves, parsley, and onion.

To make the dressing, put 2 tablespoons of the oil into a skillet, heat gently, add the pine nuts and raisins, and sauté for 3–4 minutes until the pine nuts are lightly golden. Add the Marsala and vinegar, with salt and pepper to taste, and let warm through. Stir in the remaining oil and remove from the heat.

Pour the dressing over the salad, toss lightly, and serve.

turmeric lamb
with couscous salad

Any kind of tender boneless roasting cut of lamb can be used for this recipe, but the cooking time will vary according to thickness. If you use a leg, have it boned and butterflied to lie flat on the grill.

Preheat the grill.

Put the turmeric, cinnamon, curry powder, garlic, oil, and honey into a bowl, add salt and pepper to taste, and stir well. Trim any excess fat off the lamb and rub the spice mixture all over. Transfer to a dish, cover, and chill overnight.

To make the couscous salad, put the couscous and saffron into a large bowl. Pour over 1¾ cups boiling water, mix, and set aside for 15 minutes until all the liquid has been absorbed.

Meanwhile, heat the butter and oil in a large skillet, add the onions, and cook for 8 minutes until golden and slightly frizzled. Add the garlic and cook for a further 2 minutes, then add the onions and garlic to the prepared couscous.

Add the pistachio nuts, lemon zest and juice, cilantro, salt, and pepper to taste, mix well, and set aside.

Cook the lamb on the hot grill for about 25 minutes for medium rare, turning frequently and basting with any extra marinade. Remove to a board, slice, and serve with the couscous salad.

Turmeric lamb

3 teaspoons ground turmeric

1 teaspoon ground cinnamon

3 teaspoons medium curry powder

2 garlic cloves, chopped

3 tablespoons olive oil

¼ cup clear honey

3 lbs. boneless lamb

sea salt and freshly ground black pepper

Couscous salad

13 oz. couscous, about 2 cups

½ teaspoon saffron threads

2 tablespoons unsalted butter

2 tablespoons olive oil

4 onions, sliced

1 garlic clove, chopped

⅔ cup shelled pistachios, coarsely chopped

grated zest and freshly squeezed juice of 2 unwaxed lemons

a large bunch of fresh cilantro, chopped

sea salt and freshly ground black pepper

Serves 8

figs with crispy prosciutto, blue cheese, and arugula

The flavors in this salad are so simple and classic, and here's the trick: get your hands on the best produce and all the hard work is done already! Have the prosciutto sliced fresh from the leg at the deli counter and you will notice the difference. You don't have to cook the prosciutto to a crisp if you prefer not to, although the crispy texture does go very well with sweet honey-flavored figs, in the same way that crispy bacon goes so well with maple syrup.

3 tablespoons light olive oil

6 thin slices of prosciutto

2 tablespoons red wine vinegar

1 teaspoon Dijon mustard

3–4 oz. arugula

6 figs, quartered

5 oz. firm blue cheese (such as Roquefort or Maytag Blue), crumbled

sea salt and freshly ground black pepper

Serves 4

Heat the olive oil in a nonstick skillet over medium heat and cook the prosciutto for 1 minute on each side, until crispy, and place on paper towels. When cool enough to handle, break the prosciutto into smaller pieces. Pour the oil from the skillet into a small bowl and add the vinegar, mustard, a pinch of sea salt, and freshly ground black pepper to taste.

Arrange the arugula on a serving plate with the fig quarters on top. Scatter over the cheese and the prosciutto pieces. Pour the dressing evenly over the salad to serve.

thai-style beef salad

Many Thai salads, as well as soups and stews, are flooded with the pungent flavors of fresh herbs, in particular Thai basil, mint, and cilantro. Thai basil is available from Asian stores, but if you can't get hold of any, you could use regular basil instead. Bok choy is also known as pak choi.

1 tablespoon Szechuan peppercorns, or black peppercorns, lightly crushed

1 teaspoon ground coriander

1 teaspoon sea salt

1 lb. beef fillet, in one piece

1 tablespoon peanut or canola oil

1 cucumber, thinly sliced

4 scallions, thinly sliced

2 baby bok choy, thinly sliced

a handful of fresh Thai basil

a handful of fresh mint

a handful of fresh cilantro leaves

Dressing

1 tablespoon palm sugar or brown sugar

1 tablespoon Thai fish sauce

2 tablespoons freshly squeezed lime juice

2 red chiles, seeded and chopped

1 garlic clove, crushed

Serves 4

Preheat the grill.

Put the peppercorns, coriander, and salt onto a plate and mix. Rub the beef all over with the oil and then put onto the plate and turn to coat with the spices.

Cook the beef on the preheated grill or a ridged stovetop grill pan for about 10 minutes, turning to brown evenly. Remove from the heat and let cool.

Meanwhile, to make the dressing, put the sugar into a saucepan, add the fish sauce and 2 tablespoons water, and heat until the sugar dissolves. Let cool, then stir in the lime juice, chiles, and garlic.

Cut the beef into thin slices and put into a large bowl. Add the cucumber, scallions, bok choy, and herbs. Pour over the dressing, toss well, then serve.

barbecues

The nut sauce, tarator, served with these leeks is found in Middle Eastern cooking, although it would traditionally be made with ground almonds or walnuts instead of toasted macadamia nuts. The sauce can be made in advance, but make sure that you whisk it well before using.

charred leeks
with tarator sauce

1 1/2 lbs. baby leeks, trimmed

2–3 tablespoons extra virgin olive oil

sea salt

a few lemon wedges, to serve

Tarator sauce

2 oz. macadamia nuts, toasted

1 oz. fresh bread crumbs, 1/2 cup

2 garlic cloves, crushed

1/2 cup extra virgin olive oil

1 tablespoon freshly squeezed lemon juice

sea salt and freshly ground black pepper

Serves 4

Preheat the grill.

To make the sauce, put the nuts into a food processor and grind coarsely, then add the bread crumbs, garlic, salt, and pepper. Process again to form a smooth paste. Transfer to a bowl and very gradually whisk in the olive oil, lemon juice, and 2 tablespoons boiling water to form a sauce. Season to taste with salt and pepper.

Brush the leeks with a little olive oil, season with salt, and cook over medium-hot coals for 6–10 minutes, turning occasionally, until charred and tender.

Transfer to a serving plate, sprinkle with olive oil, then pour the sauce over the top, and serve with the lemon wedges.

grilled zucchini

8 zucchini, cut lengthwise into 1/2-inch slices

olive oil

balsamic vinegar

sea salt and freshly ground black pepper

Serves 8

Preheat the grill. Cook the zucchini slices over medium heat for 3–4 minutes on each side, until lightly charred. Remove to a plate and sprinkle with oil, vinegar, salt, and pepper. Serve hot, warm, or cold.

grilled dill polenta
with lemon, fennel, and scallions

Polenta provides a good base for the flavors of this dish. There are three ingredients that fennel should possibly never be without: lemon, olive oil, and dill. Don't worry if you don't have any fresh dill—chop up the feathery fronds from the top of the fennel and use them instead.

3 tablespoons unsalted butter

1 tablespoon olive oil

1½ cups polenta or yellow cornmeal, about 8 oz.

1½ oz. Parmesan cheese, grated, plus extra to serve

a handful of fresh dill, coarsely chopped

grated zest of ½ unwaxed lemon

sea salt and freshly ground black pepper

Marinated fennel

2 tablespoons sherry or red wine vinegar

3 tablespoons olive oil

2 garlic cloves, crushed

2 bulbs of fennel, tough outer leaves removed, remainder sliced

sea salt and freshly ground black pepper

Marinated scallions

8 scallions

1 tablespoon sherry or red wine vinegar

1 tablespoon olive oil

sea salt and freshly ground black pepper

a jelly roll pan, 12 x 10 inches, lightly greased

a cookie cutter, 3 ½ inches diameter

Serves 4

To make the polenta, melt the butter and olive oil in a saucepan. Add 5 cups water and bring to a boil. Pour in the polenta in a steady stream, whisking all the time. Continue to cook, according to the package instructions, until the grainy texture has disappeared. Stir in the Parmesan, dill, salt, and pepper. Spoon into the prepared jelly roll pan, then let cool until firm.

To marinate the fennel, put the vinegar, olive oil, garlic, salt, and pepper in a bowl and mix well. Add the fennel and set aside to develop the flavors.

To marinate the scallions, put the scallions, vinegar, olive oil, salt, and pepper in a separate bowl and set aside.

Preheat the grill.

Cut out rounds of polenta with the cookie cutter. Cook on the preheated grill for 5 minutes on each side, until browned.

Add the fennel to the grill. Cook for 5–10 minutes until browned on both sides and tender. While the fennel is cooking, add the scallions and cook for 2–3 minutes until lightly blackened.

Serve the polenta piled high with fennel and scallions and sprinkle with Parmesan, lemon zest, and sea salt. Pour any remaining marinade juices over the top.

tofu
in a hot, sweet, and spicy infusion

Tofu receives some bad press and it can be exceedingly dull and tasteless when served au naturel. However, it does act as a sponge for marinades. The flavors of a marinade percolate all the way through, giving the tofu a fantastic extra lease of life and great versatility. For vegetarians, it is an excellent source of protein and, for meat-eaters, a welcome fat-free alternative.

8 oz. firm tofu

2 tablespoons hoisin sauce

3 tablespoons soy sauce

1 red chile, finely chopped

1 inch fresh ginger, peeled and grated

1 teaspoon sesame oil

1 tablespoon rice vinegar

a handful of fresh cilantro, coarsely chopped, to serve

Serves 4

Cut through the cake of tofu horizontally to make 2 thin slices. Cut each slice into 4 pieces.

Put the hoisin, soy sauce, chile, ginger, sesame oil, and rice vinegar in a bowl and mix well. Pour onto a large plate, then put the tofu on top. Spoon some of the mixture over the top so that the tofu is completely covered. Leave for as long as possible to soak up the flavors, at least 2 hours or overnight.

Preheat the grill.

Put the tofu on the preheated grill, reserving some of the marinade. Cook each side for 4–5 minutes until lightly browned. Serve immediately with the reserved marinade, topped with cilantro.

Bury foil-wrapped potatoes in the embers of a fireworks party bonfire and then enjoy jacket potatoes cooked to perfection—crispy skins with soft, fluffy insides—by the time the fireworks are over.

ember-roasted potatoes

4 medium baking potatoes

salted butter, to serve

sea salt and freshly ground black pepper

Serves 4

Wrap the potatoes individually in a double layer of foil and, as soon as the coals are glowing red, put the potatoes on top. Rake the charcoal up and around them, but without covering them. Let cook for about 25 minutes, then using tongs, turn the potatoes over carefully and cook for a further 25–30 minutes until cooked through.

Remove from the heat and carefully remove the foil, then cut the potatoes in half. Serve, topped with a spoonful of butter, salt, and pepper.

Variation For ember-roasted sweet potatoes, follow the same method but cook for about 20 minutes on each side.

eggplant and smoked cheese rolls

Truly at home in both Middle Eastern and Mediterranean cuisines, eggplants are compatible with endless spices, herbs, and a multitude of other ingredients. In this dish, they soak up the fragrance of spices and are paired with smoked cheese, enhancing the already smoky grilled flavor.

Arrange the eggplant slices on a large tray. Mix the chili and olive oils, cumin, garlic, chile, mint, salt, and pepper in a measuring cup, then pour over the eggplant slices. Turn each slice over so that both sides are well coated. Cover with plastic wrap and set aside for a few hours or overnight to soak up all the flavors.

Preheat the grill.

Put the eggplant slices on the preheated grill. Cook for about 4 minutes, then turn and cook the other side until tender and browned.

Remove from the heat, put some of the cheese at one end of a slice of eggplant, and roll up firmly (do this while the eggplant is still hot so the cheese melts). Repeat with the other slices. Sprinkle with the cilantro and lemon juice, then serve.

2 eggplants, cut lengthwise into about 5 slices each

1 teaspoon chili oil

1/2 cup olive oil

1 tablespoon cumin seeds, lightly toasted in a dry skillet and ground

2 garlic cloves, crushed

1 red chile, seeded and finely chopped

a large handful of fresh mint leaves, finely chopped

8 oz. firm smoked cheese, sliced

sea salt and freshly ground black pepper

a large handful of fresh cilantro, coarsely chopped, to serve

freshly squeezed juice of 1/2 lemon, to serve

Makes 10 rolls

Fatoush is a salad made with grilled pita bread. It's often served with halloumi, a firm cheese that can be grilled. Here is a version made with fresh mozzarella, which can also be cooked on a grill, picking up an appealing smokiness in the process.

grilled pita salad
with olive salsa and mozzarella

8 oz. fresh mozzarella cheese, drained

1 large green bell pepper, seeded and chopped

1 Lebanese (mini) cucumber, chopped

2 ripe tomatoes, chopped

1/2 red onion, finely chopped

2 pita breads

1/4 cup extra virgin olive oil

freshly squeezed juice of 1/2 lemon

sea salt and freshly ground black pepper

Olive salsa

3 oz. Kalamata olives, pitted and chopped

1 tablespoon chopped fresh parsley

1 small garlic clove, finely chopped

1/4 cup extra virgin olive oil

1 tablespoon freshly squeezed lemon juice

freshly ground black pepper

Serves 4

Preheat the grill. Squeeze the mozzarella to remove excess water, then cut into thick slices. Brush the slices well with olive oil. Cook over the hot coals for 1 minute on each side until the cheese is charred with lines and beginning to soften. Alternatively, slice the cheese and use without grilling.

Put the green bell pepper, cucumber, tomatoes, and onions into a bowl. Toast the pita breads over hot coals, cool slightly, then tear into bite-size pieces. Add to the bowl, then pour over a spoonful or two of the olive oil and a little lemon juice. Season and stir well.

Put all the ingredients for the olive salsa into a bowl and stir well.

Spoon the salad onto appetizer plates, top with a few slices of mozzarella and some olive salsa, then serve.

For this dish, you need beets and pearl onions of roughly the same size, so they will cook evenly on the grill. It is an excellent accompaniment to meats or salads.

beet and pearl onion brochettes

32 large fresh bay leaves

20 small beets

20 pearl onions, unpeeled

3 tablespoons extra virgin olive oil

1 tablespoon balsamic vinegar

sea salt and freshly ground black pepper

8 metal skewers

Serves 4

Put the bay leaves into a bowl, cover with cold water, and let soak for 1 hour.

Cut the stalks off the beets and wash well under cold running water. Put the beets and pearl onions into a large saucepan of lightly salted boiling water and blanch for 5 minutes. Drain and refresh under cold running water. Pat dry with paper towels, then peel the onions.

Preheat the grill.

Thread the beets, onions, and damp bay leaves onto the skewers, sprinkle with the olive oil and vinegar, and season well with salt and pepper. Barbecue over medium-hot coals for 20–25 minutes, turning occasionally, until charred and tender, then serve.

This is just the ticket for those who don't eat meat but love a good burger. The onion jam can be made in advance and kept in the refrigerator for several days.

mushroom burgers
with onion jam

To make the onion jam, heat the olive oil in a saucepan, add the onions, and sauté gently for 15 minutes or until very soft. Add a pinch of salt, the red currant jelly, vinegar, and 2 tablespoons water and cook for a further 15 minutes or until the mixture is glossy with a jam-like consistency. Remove from the heat and let cool.

Preheat the grill.

Brush the olive oil over the mushrooms, season well with salt and pepper, and barbecue, stem side down, for 5 minutes. Flip and barbecue for a further 5 minutes until the mushrooms are tender.

Toast the bun halves for a few minutes on the grill and fill with the mushrooms, salad leaves, onion jam, and a spoonful of mayonnaise.

2 tablespoons extra virgin olive oil

4 large portobello mushrooms, stems trimmed

4 hamburger buns, split in half

salad leaves

mayonnaise, to serve

sea salt and freshly ground black pepper

Onion jam

2 tablespoons olive oil

2 red onions, thinly sliced

1/4 cup red currant jelly

1 tablespoon red wine vinegar

Serves 4

20 uncooked shrimp

8 oz. beef tenderloin

dipping sauces, to serve

Shrimp marinade

1 teaspoon coriander seeds

1/2 teaspoon cumin seeds

1 garlic clove, crushed

1 teaspoon peeled and grated fresh ginger

2 kaffir lime leaves, shredded

1 teaspoon ground turmeric

1 tablespoon light soy sauce

1/4 cup coconut milk

1/2 teaspoon salt

Beef marinade

1 garlic clove, crushed

2 stalks of lemongrass, trimmed and finely chopped

1 tablespoon peeled and grated fresh ginger

4 cilantro roots, finely chopped

1 red chile, finely chopped

grated zest and freshly squeezed juice of 1 unwaxed lime

1 tablespoon Thai fish sauce

1 tablespoon dark soy sauce

1 1/2 tablespoons sugar

1 tablespoon sesame oil

freshly ground black pepper

40 wooden skewers, soaked in water for 30 minutes

Serves 4

Satays are found all over Southeast Asia. They are very easy to make and taste simply wonderful.

shrimp and beef satays

Shell and devein the shrimp, wash them under cold running water, and pat dry with paper towels. Put them into a shallow dish.

To make the shrimp marinade, toast the coriander and cumin seeds in a dry skillet over medium heat until golden and aromatic. Remove, let cool slightly, then transfer to a spice grinder. Add the garlic, ginger, and lime leaves, and grind to a coarse paste. Alternatively, use a pestle and mortar.

Transfer to a bowl, add the turmeric, soy sauce, coconut milk, and salt, and mix well. Pour over the shrimp and let marinate in the refrigerator for 1 hour.

To make the beef satays, cut the beef across the grain into thin strips. Mix all the beef marinade ingredients in a shallow dish, add the beef strips, turn to coat, and let marinate for about 1 hour.

Preheat the grill.

To assemble the beef satays, thread the beef strips onto the skewers, zig-zagging back and forth as you go. To assemble the shrimp satays, thread the shrimp lengthwise onto the skewers.

Barbecue both kinds of satays over hot coals for 2 minutes on each side, brushing the beef marinade over the beef satays halfway through. Serve hot with your choice of dipping sauces.

Piri-piri, a Portuguese chili condiment traditionally used to baste broiled chicken, is a combination of chopped red chile peppers, olive oil, and vinegar. It is generally very hot and only a little is needed to add spice to the food. The sauce in this recipe is not particularly hot, but you can use more chiles if you like it spicier. It works very well with squid.

squid piri-piri

To prepare the squid, put the squid body on a board and, using a sharp knife, cut down one side and open the tube out flat. Scrape away any remaining insides and wash and dry well.

Skewer each opened-out tube with 2 skewers, running them up the long sides of each piece. Rub a little salt over each one and squeeze over the lemon juice. Marinate in the refrigerator for 30 minutes.

Meanwhile, to make the piri-piri, finely chop the whole chiles without seeding them, and transfer to a small jar or bottle. Add the oil, vinegar, and a little salt and pepper. Shake well and set aside.

Preheat the grill until hot.

Baste the squid with a little of the piri-piri and barbecue for 1–1½ minutes on each side until charred. Drizzle with extra sauce and serve with lemon wedges.

* If the squid includes the tentacles, cut them off in one piece, thread with a skewer, and cook and marinate in the same way as the bodies.

8 medium squid bodies, about 8 oz. each*

freshly squeezed juice of 1 lemon, plus extra lemon wedges, to serve

sea salt

Piri-piri sauce

8 small red chiles

1¼ cups extra virgin olive oil

1 tablespoon white wine vinegar

sea salt and freshly ground black pepper

16 wooden skewers, soaked in water for 30 minutes

Serves 4

Meat and fish (the old-fashioned surf 'n' turf) can work well and this recipe is a perfect example of this balance of strong flavors. Here, chorizo sausage that needs cooking has been used, rather than the cured tapas variety, but either would do.

shrimp, chorizo, and sage skewers

10 oz. uncooked chorizo

24 large, uncooked, peeled shrimp, deveined

24 large fresh sage leaves

extra virgin olive oil

a squeeze of fresh lemon juice

freshly ground black pepper

12 wooden skewers, soaked in water for 30 minutes

Serves 6

Cut the chorizo into 24 slices about ½ inch thick and thread onto the skewers, alternating with the shrimp and sage leaves. Put a little olive oil and lemon juice into a small bowl or pitcher, mix well, then drizzle over the skewers. Sprinkle with pepper.

Preheat the grill until hot.

Barbecue the skewers for 1½–2 minutes on each side until the chorizo and shrimp are cooked through. Serve at once.

2 spicy uncooked chorizo sausages

20 freshly shucked oysters

Shallot vinegar

3 tablespoons red wine vinegar

2 tablespoons finely chopped shallots

1 tablespoon chopped fresh chives

sea salt and freshly ground black pepper

toothpicks

a large platter filled with a layer of ice cubes

Serves 4

This combination may sound slightly unusual, but it is, in fact, totally delicious. Fresh oysters, a nibble of the spicy sausages, and a sip of chilled white wine is a taste sensation—try it, you'll be amazed.

oysters with spicy chorizo

To make the shallot vinegar, put the ingredients into a bowl and mix well. Pour into a small dish and set aside until required.

Preheat the grill.

Barbecue the sausages over hot coals for 8–10 minutes or until cooked through. Cut the sausages into bite-size pieces and spike them onto toothpicks. Arrange in the center of a large ice-filled platter. Put the oysters on their half-shells and arrange on top of the ice. Serve with the shallot vinegar.

Chunks of swordfish coated in a spicy rub, then barbecued on skewers and served with fluffy couscous, make the perfect alfresco lunch.

moroccan fish skewers
with couscous

1 1/2 lbs. swordfish steak

extra virgin olive oil

24 large bay leaves, soaked in cold water for 1 hour

2 lemons, cut into 24 chunks

freshly squeezed lemon juice, to serve

Moroccan rub

1 1/2 teaspoons coriander seeds

1/2 teaspoon cumin seeds

1 cinnamon stick

1/2 teaspoon whole allspice berries

3 cloves

1/2 teaspoon ground turmeric

1 teaspoon dried onion flakes

1/2 teaspoon sea salt

1/4 teaspoon paprika

Couscous

10 oz. couscous, 1 1/2 cups

1 1/4 cups boiling water

2 oz. freshly grated Parmesan cheese, 1/2 cup

4 tablespoons unsalted butter, melted

1 tablespoon chopped fresh thyme

sea salt and freshly ground black pepper

8 wooden skewers, soaked in water for 30 minutes

Serves 4

To make the Moroccan rub, toast the whole spices in a dry skillet over medium heat for about 1–2 minutes or until golden and aromatic. Remove from the heat and let cool. Transfer to a spice grinder and crush to a coarse powder. Put the spices into a bowl, add the remaining ingredients, and mix well. Set aside to infuse.

Using a sharp knife, cut the swordfish into 32 cubes and put into a shallow ceramic dish. Add a sprinkle of olive oil and the Moroccan rub, and toss well until the fish is evenly coated. Marinate in the refrigerator for 1 hour.

About 10 minutes before cooking the fish, put the couscous into a bowl. Pour the boiling water over the couscous. Let plump for a few minutes, then fluff with a fork. Transfer the couscous to a warmed serving dish and immediately stir in the Parmesan cheese, melted butter, thyme, salt, and pepper. Keep the couscous warm.

Preheat the grill. Thread the fish, bay leaves, and chunks of lemon onto the soaked wooden skewers and barbecue over hot coals for 3–4 minutes, turning halfway through until cooked. Serve the skewers on a bed of couscous, sprinkled with a little olive oil and lemon juice.

swordfish with salsa

Swordfish is brought to life with this delicious salsa. Slow-roasting softens the tomatoes and intensifies their flavor. This salsa is great served with many different fish and meat dishes, as well as on a bowl of fresh pasta such as ravioli.

1 lb. cherry tomatoes

2 red onions, finely chopped

1/2 teaspoon red pepper flakes

a large bunch of fresh flatleaf parsley, chopped

1/3 cup olive oil

freshly squeezed juice of 2 limes

8 swordfish steaks, 4 oz. each

sea salt and freshly ground pepper

Serves 8

Preheat the oven to 300°F.

To make the salsa, put the tomatoes into a roasting pan and cook in the preheated oven for 1 hour. Remove and let cool.

Transfer to a bowl, add the onions, pepper flakes, parsley, oil, lime juice, salt, and pepper. Mix well.

Preheat the grill.

Sprinkle the swordfish steaks with salt and pepper. Cook over medium heat on the preheated grill for 4–6 minutes on each side, depending on thickness, until just cooked through. Serve with the salsa.

sesame-crusted marlin
with ginger dressing

Marlin is fantastic for the outdoor grill, as it is firm and doesn't break up when turned. It's a dense fish with an intense flavor, so serve it in small portions. Swordfish also works well.

20 marlin or swordfish steaks, about 4 oz. each

5 egg whites

1¹/₂ lbs. toasted sesame seeds

1 tablespoon red pepper flakes

Ginger dressing

14 oz. fresh ginger, peeled and finely chopped

2³/₄ cups light soy sauce

2 bunches of scallions, chopped

¹/₄ cup sesame oil

Serves 20

Preheat the grill.

To make the dressing, put the ginger, soy sauce, scallions, and sesame oil into a bowl and mix.

Dry the marlin steaks with paper towels. Put the egg whites into a bowl and whisk until frothy. Put the sesame seeds and red pepper flakes onto a large plate and mix. Dip each marlin steak first into the egg whites, then into the sesame seeds and pepper flakes, until evenly coated on both sides.

Cook on the preheated grill for 5 minutes on each side. Spoon the dressing over the marlin and serve.

Even if the snapper has already been scaled at the fish counter, go over it again to remove any stray scales—they are huge! A fish grilling basket could also be used to cook this fish. Serve with chilled, crisp white or rosé wine and crusty bread.

red snapper with parsley salad

To make the herb, lemon, and garlic marinade, strip the rosemary and thyme leaves from the stalk and put into a mortar. Add the bay leaves, garlic, and lemon zest and pound with a pestle to release the aromas. Put the mixture into a bowl and add the peppercorns and olive oil.

Using a sharp knife, cut several slashes into each side of the fish. Put into a shallow ceramic dish and add the marinade. Marinate in the refrigerator for 4 hours, but return to room temperature 1 hour before cooking.

Preheat the grill.

Just before cooking the fish, make the salad. Put the raisins into a bowl, add the verjuice, and let soak for 15 minutes. Drain and set the liquid aside. Put the parsley, pine nuts, soaked raisins, and feta into a bowl. Put the olive oil, vinegar, and reserved raisin liquid into a separate bowl and mix well. Pour over the salad and toss until the leaves are well coated. Season with sea salt and black pepper.

Grill the fish over hot coals for 4–5 minutes on each side, let rest briefly, and serve at once with the parsley salad.

* Verjuice, which is used in the salad dressing, is produced from the juice of unripe grapes. It is available from Italian gourmet stores. If you can't find it, use white grape juice instead.

4 red snapper, cleaned and well scaled, about 8 oz. each

Herb, lemon, and garlic marinade

2 sprigs of fresh rosemary

2 sprigs of fresh thyme

4 bay leaves

2 large garlic cloves, coarsely chopped

grated zest of 1 unwaxed lemon

1 teaspoon cracked black peppercorns

1 cup extra virgin olive oil

Parsley salad

1/3 cup raisins

2 tablespoons verjuice* or white grape juice

leaves from a large bunch of fresh parsley

1/4 cup pine nuts

2 oz. feta cheese, crumbled

3 tablespoons extra virgin olive oil

2 teaspoons balsamic vinegar

sea salt and freshly ground black pepper

Serves 4

Smoking food on the grill is done using the indirect barbecuing method, so the food cooks more slowly and the flavor of the smoke can penetrate. For smoking, you will need a grill with a lid.

hot-smoked creole salmon

4 salmon fillets, skinned, about 8 oz. each

Creole rub

1/2 small onion, finely chopped

1 garlic clove, finely chopped

1 tablespoon chopped fresh thyme

1 tablespoon paprika

1 teaspoon ground cumin

1 teaspoon sea salt

1/4 teaspoon cayenne pepper

1 tablespoon brown sugar

freshly ground black pepper

Mango and sesame salsa

1 large ripe mango, peeled, pitted, and chopped

4 scallions, chopped

1 fresh red chile, seeded and chopped

1 garlic clove, crushed

1 tablespoon light soy sauce

1 tablespoon freshly squeezed lime juice

1 teaspoon sesame oil

1/2 tablespoon sugar

1 tablespoon chopped fresh cilantro

sea salt and freshly ground black pepper

a large handful of wood chips, such as hickory, soaked in water for 1 hour, then drained

Serves 4

To make the Creole rub, put all the ingredients into a small bowl, stir well, and set aside to infuse until ready to use.

Wash the salmon under cold running water and pat dry with paper towels. Using tweezers, pull out any bones, then put the fish into a dish and work the Creole rub all over it. Marinate in the refrigerator for at least 1 hour.

To make the salsa, put the chopped mango into a bowl, then add the scallions, chile, garlic, soy sauce, lime juice, sesame oil, sugar, cilantro, salt, and pepper. Mix well and set aside for 30 minutes to let the flavors infuse.

Preheat the charcoal grill for indirect barbecuing, according to the manufacturer's instructions. Put a drip tray in the middle and, when the coals are hot, tip half the soaked wood chips onto each pile. Cover with the lid, leaving any air vents open during barbecuing.

As soon as the wood chips start to smoke, put the salmon fillets into the center of the grill, cover, and cook for about 15–20 minutes or until the salmon is cooked through.

To test the fish, press the salmon with your finger—the flesh should feel firm and start to open into flakes. Serve hot or cold, with the mango and sesame salsa.

A great way to prepare whole salmon is to remove the central bone from the fish, then tie the two fillets back together. If your filleting skills are limited, ask your fish seller to fillet the whole fish for you.

whole salmon
stuffed with herbs

4 lbs. whole salmon, filleted

1 stick salted butter, softened

1 cup chopped, fresh soft-leaf mixed herbs, such as basil, chives, mint, parsley, and tarragon

grated zest of 1 unwaxed lemon

1 garlic clove, crushed

sea salt and freshly ground black pepper

olive oil, for brushing

Serves 8

Preheat the grill.

Put the salmon fillets flat onto a board, flesh side up. Carefully pull out any remaining bones with tweezers.

Put the butter, herbs, lemon zest, garlic, and plenty of pepper into a small bowl and beat well. Spread the mixture over one of the salmon fillets and put the second on the top, arranging them top to tail.

Using kitchen twine, tie the fish together at 1-inch intervals. Brush with a little olive oil, season, and cook on the flat plate of the preheated grill for 10 minutes on each side. Let rest for a further 10 minutes. Remove the twine and serve the fish cut into portions.

peppered tuna steak
with salsa rossa

Salsa rossa is one of those divine Italian sauces that transforms simple meat and fish dishes into food nirvana. The slight sweetness from the bell peppers is a good foil for the spicy pepper crust.

1/3 cup mixed peppercorns, coarsely crushed

6 tuna steaks, 8 oz. each

1 tablespoon extra virgin olive oil

salad greens, to serve

Salsa rossa

1 large red bell pepper

1 tablespoon extra virgin olive oil

2 garlic cloves, crushed

2 large ripe tomatoes, peeled and coarsely chopped

a small pinch of red pepper flakes

1 tablespoon dried oregano

1 tablespoon red wine vinegar

sea salt and freshly ground black pepper

Serves 6

To make the salsa rossa, broil the bell pepper until charred all over, then put into a plastic bag and let cool. Remove and discard the skin and seeds, reserving any juices, then chop the flesh.

Put the oil into a skillet, heat gently, then add the garlic and sauté for 3 minutes. Add the tomatoes, pepper flakes, and oregano and simmer gently for 15 minutes. Stir in the peppers and the vinegar and simmer for a further 5 minutes to evaporate any excess liquid.

Transfer to a blender and purée until fairly smooth. Add salt and pepper to taste and let cool. It may be stored in a screw-top jar in the refrigerator for up to 3 days.

Put the crushed peppercorns onto a large plate. Brush the tuna steaks with olive oil, then press the crushed peppercorns into the surface. Preheat the grill until hot, add the tuna, and cook for 1 minute on each side. Wrap loosely in foil and let rest for 5 minutes before serving with the salsa rossa and a salad of mixed leaves.

Dukkah is a spicy, crunchy condiment comprising mixed nuts and spices, which are ground to a coarse powder and served as a dip for warm bread. For this recipe, it is used as a coating for barbecued tuna. Preserved lemons are available from French, North African, and good gourmet stores.

dukkah crusted tuna
with preserved lemon salsa

4 tuna steaks, about 8 oz. each

3 tablespoons sesame seeds

2 tablespoons coriander seeds

1/2 tablespoon cumin seeds

1/4 cup blanched almonds, chopped

1/2 teaspoon salt

freshly ground black pepper

olive oil, for brushing

Preserved lemon salsa

1 preserved lemon

1/4 cup sun-dried tomatoes

2 scallions, very finely chopped

1 tablespoon coarsely chopped fresh parsley

3 tablespoons extra virgin olive oil

1/4 teaspoon sugar

Serves 4

To make the salsa, chop the preserved lemon and tomatoes finely and put into a bowl. Stir in the scallions, parsley, olive oil, and sugar and set aside until ready to serve.

Preheat the grill.

Wash the tuna steaks under cold running water and pat dry with paper towels.

Put the sesame seeds into a dry skillet and toast over medium heat until golden and aromatic. Remove and let cool. Repeat with the coriander seeds, cumin seeds, and almonds. Transfer to a spice grinder and grind coarsely. Alternatively, use a pestle and mortar. Add the salt and a little pepper.

Brush the tuna steaks with olive oil and coat with the spicy nut mixture. Cook over hot coals for 1 minute on each side, top with the salsa, and serve.

Cooking with the lid on your grill creates the same effect as cooking in a conventional oven. If you don't have a grill with a lid, you can cut the chicken in half and cook on the grill rack for about 15 minutes on each side.

whole chicken
roasted on the grill

3 lbs. chicken

1 lemon, halved

4 garlic cloves, peeled

a small bunch of fresh thyme

extra virgin olive oil

sea salt and freshly ground black pepper

Serves 4–6

Wash the chicken thoroughly under cold running water and pat dry with paper towels.

Rub the chicken all over with the halved lemon, then put the lemon halves inside the body cavity with the garlic cloves and thyme. Rub a little olive oil into the skin and season liberally with salt and pepper.

Preheat the grill for indirect barbecuing, following the manufacturer's instructions, and put a drip tray in the middle. Brush the grill rack with oil and put the chicken above the drip tray. Cover with the lid, then cook over medium-hot coals for 1 hour or until the skin is golden, the flesh is cooked through, and the juices run clear when the thickest part of the meat is pierced with a skewer. If any bloody juices appear, then cook a little longer.

Let the chicken rest for 10 minutes before serving.

pepper 'n' spice chicken

Based on the classic Asian salt 'n' pepper squid, this delicious dish is a great way to use up leftover chicken. Serve with a squeeze of lime and the sweet chili sauce.

1 small chicken

2 tablespoons toasted sesame oil

1–2 limes, cut into wedges

Fragrant Asian rub

4 whole star anise

2 teaspoons Szechuan peppercorns

1 teaspoon fennel seeds

2 small pieces of cassia bark or 1 cinnamon stick, broken

6 cloves

2 garlic cloves, finely chopped

grated zest of 2 unwaxed limes

1 teaspoon sea salt

Sweet chili sauce

6 large red chiles, seeded and chopped

4 garlic cloves, chopped

1 teaspoon peeled and grated fresh ginger

1 teaspoon sea salt

1/2 cup rice wine vinegar

1/2 cup sugar

Serves 4

To make the fragrant Asian rub, toast the whole spices in a dry skillet over medium heat for 1–2 minutes or until golden and aromatic. Remove from the heat and let cool. Transfer to a spice grinder and crush to a coarse powder. Put the spices into a bowl, add the garlic, lime zest, and salt, and mix well. Set aside to infuse until ready to use.

To make the sweet chili sauce, put the chiles, garlic, ginger, and salt into a food processor and blend to a coarse paste. Transfer to a saucepan, add the vinegar and sugar, bring to a boil, and simmer gently, partially covered, for 5 minutes until the mixture becomes a thin syrup. Remove from the heat and let cool.

Cut the chicken into 12 pieces and put into a dish. Add the rub and sesame oil and work well into the chicken pieces. Marinate in the refrigerator for 2 hours, but return to room temperature for 1 hour before cooking.

Preheat the grill, then cook the chicken over medium-hot coals for 15–20 minutes, turning after 10 minutes, until the chicken is cooked through and the juices run clear when the thickest part of the meat is pierced with a skewer. Squeeze with lime juice, let cool slightly, and serve with the sweet chili sauce.

2 duck breast fillets, with skin, about 8 oz. each

1 tablespoon salt

2 tablespoons honey

2 tablespoons dark soy sauce

1/2 teaspoon ground star anise

12 package Vietnamese rice paper wrappers

1/2 cucumber, cut into strips

a few fresh herb leaves,
such as cilantro, mint, and Thai basil

Asian barbecue sauce

1/2 cup crushed tomatoes

2 tablespoons hoisin sauce

1 teaspoon hot chili sauce

2 garlic cloves, crushed

2 tablespoons sweet soy sauce

1 tablespoon rice wine vinegar

1 teaspoon ground coriander

1/2 teaspoon ground cinnamon

1/4 teaspoon Chinese five-spice pepper

Serves 4

This dish is similar to the famous Peking duck but takes much less time to prepare. Cooking duck on an outdoor grill is best done by the indirect method, where the coals are pushed to the sides and a drip tray placed underneath to catch the fat.

grilled duck rice paper rolls

To make the Asian barbecue sauce, put all the ingredients into a small saucepan, add ½ cup water, bring to a boil, and simmer gently for 10 minutes. Remove from the heat and let cool. Pour into an airtight container and store in the refrigerator for up to 2 weeks.

Using a sharp knife, cut several slashes into the duck skin. Rub the skin with the salt and put into a shallow dish. Put the honey, soy sauce, and ground star anise into a bowl and mix well. Pour over the duck. Let marinate in a cool place for at least 1 hour.

Set up the grill for indirect barbecuing, following the manufacturer's instructions, and put a drip tray in the middle. Cook the duck breast for 15 minutes or until well browned and firm to the touch, let rest for 5 minutes, then cut into thin strips and set aside until required.

Put the rice paper wrappers into a large bowl of cold water, let soak until softened, then pat dry and spread flat on the work surface. Put a few slices of duck, some strips of cucumber, and herbs into the center of each wrapper and add a little of the barbecue sauce.

Fold the ends of the wrapper over the duck and roll up the sides to enclose the filling. Transfer to a large platter and serve with the barbecue sauce.

A good burger should be thick, moist, tender, and juicy. These lamb burgers are all that and more. Serve in crusty rolls with a few slices of tomato, plenty of fresh salad greens, and a generous spoonful of the cool minty yogurt dressing. The perfect burger for a patio picnic.

lamb burgers with mint yogurt

1¹/₂ lbs. boneless lamb shoulder, cut into ¹/₂-inch cubes

4 oz. salt pork, chopped

1 onion, very finely chopped

2 garlic cloves, crushed

2 tablespoons ground cumin

2 teaspoons ground cinnamon

1 tablespoon dried oregano

2 teaspoons salt

¹/₂ cup fresh bread crumbs

1 tablespoon capers, drained and chopped

freshly ground black pepper

1 extra large egg, beaten

4 crusty rolls, to serve

salad leaves, to serve

tomato slices, to serve

Mint yogurt

8 oz. plain yogurt

2 tablespoons chopped fresh mint

sea salt and freshly ground black pepper

Serves 4

Put the lamb and pork into a food processor and process briefly until coarsely ground. Transfer to a bowl and, using your hands, work in the chopped onion, garlic, cumin, cinnamon, oregano, salt, bread crumbs, capers, pepper, and beaten egg. Cover and marinate in the refrigerator for at least 2 hours.

Preheat the grill.

Put the yogurt into a bowl and stir in the mint, then add a little salt and pepper to taste. Set aside until required.

Using damp hands, shape the meat into 8 burgers. Brush the grill rack with oil. Barbecue the burgers for about 3 minutes on each side.

Split the rolls in half and fill with the cooked burgers, salad greens, tomato slices, and a spoonful of mint yogurt.

Variation For a traditional hamburger, replace the lamb with beef, omit the spices, and, instead of the capers, add 4 chopped anchovy fillets. Serve in hamburger buns with salad.

Souvlaki is the classic Greek kabob, a delicious combination of cubed lamb marinated in red wine with herbs and lemon juice—a juicy and succulent dish.

souvlaki
with cracked wheat salad

2 lbs. boneless lamb, such as shoulder

1 tablespoon chopped fresh rosemary

1 tablespoon dried oregano

1 onion, chopped

4 garlic cloves, chopped

1 1/4 cups red wine

freshly squeezed juice of 1 lemon

1/3 cup olive oil

sea salt and freshly ground black pepper

Cracked wheat salad

3 1/4 cups cracked wheat (bulgur wheat)

1 cup chopped fresh flatleaf parsley

1/2 cup chopped fresh mint leaves

2 garlic cloves, crushed

1/2 cup extra virgin olive oil

freshly squeezed juice of 2 lemons

a pinch of sugar

sea salt and and freshly ground black pepper

6 large rosemary stalks or metal skewers

Serves 6

Trim any large pieces of fat from the lamb then cut the meat into 1-inch cubes. Put into a shallow, non-metal dish. Add the rosemary, oregano, onion, garlic, wine, lemon juice, olive oil, salt, and pepper. Toss well, cover, and let marinate in the refrigerator for 4 hours. Return to room temperature for 1 hour before cooking.

To make the salad, soak the cracked wheat in warm water for 30 minutes until the water has been absorbed and the grains have softened. Strain well to extract any excess water and transfer the wheat to a bowl. Add all the remaining ingredients, season to taste, and set aside for 30 minutes to develop the flavors.

Preheat the grill. Thread the lamb onto the rosemary stalks. Cook on the preheated grill for 10 minutes, turning and basting from time to time. Let rest for 5 minutes, then serve with the salad.

butterflied leg of lamb
with cumin, lemon, and garlic

A butterflied leg of lamb, where the bone is removed and the meat opened up to create a huge flat piece of meat, is one of the tastiest, simplest, and most impressive dishes to barbecue. Order it in advance from a butcher and he'll do all the hard work for you. Serve with Kisir (page 40), mixed salad greens, and some flatbreads.

2 large garlic cloves, chopped

1 teaspoon sea salt

1 tablespoon cumin seeds

1 teaspoon coriander seeds

1 teaspoon herbes de Provence

1/2 teaspoon black peppercorns

1/4 teaspoon crushed chiles

freshly squeezed juice of 1 lemon

3 tablespoons olive oil

1 large butterflied leg of lamb (about 4 1/2–5 lbs.)

a large roasting pan

Serves 8

Put the garlic, salt, cumin seeds, coriander seeds, herbes de Provence, black peppercorns, and chiles in a mortar and pound with a pestle until the garlic breaks down and you have a thick paste. Gradually work in the lemon juice and olive oil. Work over the meat with a small, sharp knife, cutting away any excess fat, then cut the meat into 2 or 3 manageable pieces. Put the meat in a roasting pan, rub in the marinade, cover, and leave in a cool place for at least 2 hours.

Preheat the grill.

Barbecue the lamb for 15–20 minutes, depending on the thickness of the meat and your preference, turning it halfway through the cooking time. Remove to a warmed carving plate, cover with foil, and let rest for 15 minutes before slicing thinly.

1¼ lbs. ground pork

5 oz. ground salt pork

⅓ cup bread crumbs

1 stalk of lemongrass, trimmed and tough outer layer discarded, very finely chopped

6 kaffir lime leaves, very thinly sliced

2 garlic cloves, crushed

1 inch fresh ginger, peeled and grated

1 fresh red chile, seeded and chopped

2 tablespoons Thai fish sauce

lettuce leaves, to serve

a handful of fresh herb leaves, such as mint, cilantro, and Thai basil, to serve

Sweet Chili Sauce (page 71), to serve

4 wooden skewers, soaked in water for 30 minutes

Serves 4

These delicious pork balls are served wrapped in a lettuce leaf with plenty of fresh herbs and a sweet chili sauce.

vietnamese pork balls

Put the pork, salt pork, and bread crumbs into a bowl, then add the lemongrass, lime leaves, garlic, ginger, chile, and fish sauce and mix well. Let marinate in the refrigerator for 1 hour.

Preheat the grill. Shape the mixture into 20 small balls and carefully thread 5 onto each of the soaked wooden skewers. Brush the grill rack with oil. Cook the skewers over hot coals for 5–6 minutes, turning halfway through, until cooked.

Serve the pork balls wrapped in the lettuce leaves with the herbs and sweet chili sauce.

An essential sauce used for the smoky spareribs recipe opposite.

barbecue sauce

1 cup crushed tomatoes

½ cup maple syrup

2 tablespoons light molasses

2 tablespoons tomato ketchup

2 tablespoons white wine vinegar

3 tablespoons Worcestershire sauce

1 tablespoon Dijon mustard

1 teaspoon garlic powder

¼ teaspoon hot paprika

sea salt and freshly ground pepper

Put all the ingredients in a small saucepan, bring to a boil, and simmer gently for 10–15 minutes until reduced slightly and thickened. Season to taste and let cool.

2¹/2 lbs. spareribs

1¹/4 cups white wine vinegar

2 tablespoons soft brown sugar

1 tablespoon salt

1 tablespoon sweet paprika

2 teaspoons crushed black pepper

2 teaspoons onion powder

1 teaspoon garlic powder

¹/4 teaspoon cayenne pepper

²/3 cup Barbecue Sauce (page 76)

coleslaw, to serve

Serves 4

These barbecued ribs are spicy, smoky, sticky, tender, and lip-smackingly good. They may take a little time to prepare because of soaking and marinating, but they are simple to cook and definitely well worth the effort.

smoky spareribs

Wash the spareribs under cold running water and pat dry with paper towels. Put the spareribs into a large dish, add the vinegar, and let soak for 4 hours or overnight. Rinse the ribs well and pat dry with paper towels.

Put the sugar, salt, paprika, pepper, onion powder, garlic powder, and cayenne into a bowl and mix well. Rub the mixture all over the spareribs and let marinate in the refrigerator for 2 hours.

Preheat the grill. Cook the ribs over low heat for 20 minutes on each side. Brush with the barbecue sauce and cook for a further 15 minutes on each side until the ribs are lightly charred, tender, and sticky. Remove and let cool briefly, then serve with coleslaw.

Ripe figs filled with goat cheese, then wrapped in prosciutto, make a great appetizer at an alfresco supper. Prepare the salad in advance, but add the dressing at the last minute, otherwise it may become soggy.

fig, goat cheese, and prosciutto skewers
with radicchio salad

Using a sharp knife, cut each fig lengthwise into quarters without cutting all the way through. Cut the cheese into 8 equal pieces, put into the middle of each fig, and close the figs. Wrap each fig with a slice of the ham and thread carefully onto the soaked wooden skewers.

Preheat the grill, then cook the skewers over medium-hot coals for 4–5 minutes, turning halfway through until the ham is browned and the figs are sizzling.

To make the salad, tear the radicchio leaves into pieces and put into a bowl with the walnuts. Put the remaining ingredients into a separate bowl and whisk well. Pour the dressing over the leaves and toss until coated. Serve with the skewers.

* To reduce balsamic vinegar, put 1¼ cups into a saucepan and boil gently until it has reduced by about two-thirds and has reached the consistency of thick syrup. Let cool, then store in a clean jar or bottle.

8 large ripe figs

3 oz. goat cheese

8 slices prosciutto

Radicchio salad

1 head of radicchio, trimmed

a handful of walnut pieces, pan-toasted

¼ cup walnut oil

2 tablespoons extra virgin olive oil

1 tablespoon vincotto or reduced balsamic vinegar*

sea salt and freshly ground black pepper

4 wooden skewers, soaked in water for 30 minutes

Serves 4

3 slices white bread

5 tablespoons milk

1¾ lbs. ground pork

2 eggs

a handful of fresh parsley, finely chopped

4 garlic cloves, crushed

1 teaspoon ground cinnamon

a large pinch of ground cloves

1 teaspoon ground turmeric

a large pinch of ground red pepper

seeds of 4 cardamom pods, crushed

1 teaspoon sea salt

freshly ground black pepper

olive oil, for brushing

tomato chutney, to serve (optional)

6 pita breads, to serve

2 cups shredded iceberg lettuce, to serve

10 oz. plain yogurt, to serve

Serves 4–6

No cook-out—especially where children are involved—is complete without burgers, but burgers don't necessarily have to mean junk food. Not only is it healthier to make your own, but fun too, as you can experiment with herbs and spices. This recipe can be varied to use beef, lamb, or poultry, but make sure that you use good-quality meat. The addition of bread to the mixture gives a smoother texture and flavor.

aromatic pork burger in pita bread

Soak the bread in the milk for 10–15 minutes until soft, then squeeze the bread with your hands until it is almost dry and put in a bowl. Add the ground pork, eggs, parsley, garlic, spices, salt, and plenty of pepper. Mix well, cover, and let stand for 60 minutes.

Shape the meat mixture into 12 patties. Cover and refrigerate until required.

Preheat the grill.

When ready to cook, brush the patties lightly with olive oil and cook them on the preheated hot grill for 20 minutes, turning them from time to time to avoid burning. Cut into one of the burgers to make sure it is cooked in the middle—if it is still pink, cook for an extra 5–10 minutes. Transfer the burgers to a plate. Spread each one with a spoonful of tomato chutney, if using.

Heat the pita breads on the grill until just warm. Cut each one in half, open, and fill with lettuce, yogurt, and a burger, then serve.

If you can't find porcini mushrooms, any large open mushroom will taste great cooked on the grill.

beef tenderloin with mushrooms

1 lb. beef tenderloin

1 tablespoon extra virgin olive oil, plus extra for brushing

1 tablespoon crushed black peppercorns

8 large porcini or portobello mushrooms

sea salt and freshly ground black pepper

Beet and Pearl Onion Brochettes (page 56), to serve (optional)

Dressing

1/2 cup extra virgin olive oil

1 garlic clove, chopped

1 tablespoon chopped fresh parsley

a squeeze of fresh lemon juice

Serves 4

Brush the meat with the olive oil, press the peppercorns into the meat, then sprinkle with salt.

Preheat the grill to high. Cook the beef for 15 minutes for rare, 20 minutes for medium, and 25 minutes for well done, turning every 5 minutes or so until evenly browned on all sides. Transfer the beef to a roasting pan, cover with foil, and let rest for 10 minutes.

Brush the mushrooms with olive oil, season with salt and pepper, then put them stem side down on the grill rack and barbecue for 5 minutes on each side. Transfer the mushrooms to the roasting pan and let rest for a further 1–2 minutes.

Meanwhile, put all the dressing ingredients into a bowl and mix well. Serve the beef in thick slices with the mushrooms, a sprinkle of the dressing, and the beet and pearl onion brochettes, if using.

best-ever beef burger

There are many burger recipes and everyone has their favorite. This one is best served in a bun, with pickles and sauce, and a simple salad of tomatoes, lettuce, and olives.

Put the ground steak and pork into a bowl and add the anchovies, bread crumbs, thyme, mustard, beaten egg, salt, and pepper, working it with your hands to make a nice, sticky mixture. Shape into 6 burgers and chill for 1 hour.

Preheat the grill. Cook the burgers on the preheated grill for about 4 minutes on each side. Remove from the heat and let rest for 5 minutes. Serve in a bun, with sautéed onions, dill pickles, and the tomato, lettuce, and olive salad, if using.

* To make the ground meat, ask your butcher to put the beef and pork through a meat grinder. Alternatively, put it into a food processor and pulse briefly to make a slightly coarse mixture..

1 1/2 lbs. sirloin steak, ground*

2 oz. skinless pork belly, ground*

8 anchovy fillets in oil, drained and finely chopped

1 cup soft white bread crumbs

2 tablespoons chopped fresh thyme

1 tablespoon wholegrain mustard

1 extra large egg, lightly beaten

sea salt and freshly ground black pepper

6 hamburger buns, split in half, to serve

sautéed onions, to serve

dill pickles, to serve

tomato, lettuce, and olive salad, to serve (optional)

Serves 6

entrées

quiche lorraine

This is the classic tart from Alsace and Lorraine, and the forerunner of many copies. Made well and with the best ingredients, this simplest of dishes is food fit for kings, especially when a little grated Gruyère is added to the filling. The quantities given for the dough are generous—any left over may be frozen or used to make tartlets. Making the dough by hand is the best method because more air will be incorporated, but if you have hot hands, the food processor is a blessing!

8 oz. bacon, chopped, or cubed prosciutto

5 eggs

3/4 cup heavy cream or crème fraîche

freshly grated nutmeg, to taste

1/2 cup grated Gruyère cheese, about 2 oz.

sea salt and freshly ground black pepper

Shortcrust pastry dough

2 cups all-purpose flour

a pinch of salt

4 1/2 tablespoons vegetable shortening or lard, chilled and diced

6 tablespoons unsalted butter, chilled and diced

2–3 tablespoons ice water

a tart pan, 9 inches diameter

baking beans

Serves 4–6

Preheat the oven to 400°F.

To make the pastry dough, sift the flour and salt together into a bowl. (Alternatively, sift into a food processor.)

Rub in the shortening and butter until the mixture resembles bread crumbs. (Or add to the food processor and blend for 30 seconds for the same result.)

Add the water, mixing lightly with a knife to bring the dough together. (Or add to the food processor, and pulse for 10 seconds until the dough forms large lumps. Add another tablespoon of water and repeat if necessary.)

Knead lightly on a floured work surface, then shape into a flattened ball, wrap in plastic wrap, and chill for at least 30 minutes before rolling out.

Bring the dough to room temperature. Roll out thinly on a lightly floured work surface and use to line the tart pan. Prick the base, chill, or freeze for 15 minutes.

Spread foil over the pan, letting it hang over the sides, then fill the pan with baking beans. Set on a baking sheet and bake blind in the center of the oven for about 10–12 minutes.

Remove the foil and baking beans, and return the pie crust to the oven for a further 5–7 minutes to dry out completely.

To prevent the crust from becoming soggy when the filling is added, brush the blind-baked crust with beaten egg. Bake again for 5–10 minutes until set and shiny. This will also fill and seal any holes made when pricking before the blind baking.

If necessary, repeat the sealing process until an impervious layer has been built. Put the crust to one side.

Heat a nonstick skillet and sauté the bacon or pancetta until brown and crisp, then drain on paper towels. Scatter over the base of the pie crust.

Put the eggs and cream into a bowl, beat well, and season with salt, pepper, and nutmeg to taste. Carefully pour the mixture over the bacon and sprinkle with the Gruyère.

Bake for about 25 minutes until just set, golden brown, and puffy. Serve warm or at room temperature.

This amazingly savory Ligurian focaccia is topped with a concentrated sauce of tomatoes, salted anchovies or salted sardines (hence the name), and whole melting cloves of garlic. It is perfect for outdoor eating, served in thin slices with a cold glass of wine or beer.

sardenaira

1 cake compressed yeast

1/2 teaspoon sugar

2/3 cup warm milk

41/4 cups Italian "00" flour or cake flour

1/3 cup extra virgin olive oil

6 tablespoons hand-hot water

2 onions, thinly sliced

21/4 lbs. fresh, very ripe tomatoes, peeled and chopped, or 21/4 lbs. (drained weight) canned whole tomatoes

31/2 oz. anchovies or sardines in salt

12 or more whole garlic cloves, unpeeled

3 oz. or more small pitted black olives

1 tablespoon dried oregano

sea salt and freshly ground black pepper

an 11 x 15 x 1 inch baking pan, oiled

Serves 10

In a large bowl, cream the compressed yeast with the sugar and whisk in the warm milk. Leave for 10 minutes until frothy.

Sift the flour with 1 teaspoon salt into a large bowl and make a well in the center. Pour in the yeast mixture, 4 tablespoons of the olive oil, and the water. Mix together with a round-bladed knife, then use your hands until the dough comes together. Tip out onto a lightly floured surface, then knead briskly for 10–15 minutes until smooth, shiny, and elastic. Try not to add any extra flour at this stage—a wetter dough is better. If you feel the dough is sticky, flour your hands and not the dough. The dough should be quite soft. If it is really too soft to handle, knead in a little more flour.

To test if the dough is ready, roll it into a fat sausage, take each end in either hand, lift the dough up, and pull and stretch the dough outward, gently wiggling it up and down—it should stretch out quite easily. If it doesn't, it needs more kneading. Shape into a neat ball. Put it in an oiled bowl, cover with plastic wrap or a damp dish towel, and let rise in a warm, draft-free place until doubled in size—about 1½ hours.

Preheat the oven to 350°F.

Heat the remaining olive oil in a large saucepan, add the onions, and cook for about 10 minutes until beginning to soften and color slightly. Add the tomatoes and cook gently until collapsed and very thick. Meanwhile, split the anchovies, remove the backbone, rinse, and roughly chop. Stir into the sauce and season to taste.

Knock back the dough, knead lightly, then stretch and pat it out into the prepared pan, pushing the dough well up the edges. Spread the sauce on top of the crust, cover with the whole garlic cloves and the olives, then sprinkle with the oregano. Drizzle with a little olive oil and bake for about 1 hour until the focaccia is golden. Serve sliced—hot, warm, or cold.

roquefort and walnut tart

Blue cheese imparts a wonderful richness of flavor to this light, creamy tart with walnut crust. Served with a salad made from arugula, pears, and walnuts, it is a delicious entrée for an alfresco lunch.

To make the pastry dough, put the walnuts into a dry skillet and cook for 1–2 minutes until they start to smell toasted. Transfer to a bowl and let cool.

Transfer to a food processor or blender and grind to a meal. Sift the flour and salt into a bowl and rub in the butter until the mixture resembles fine bread crumbs. Stir in the ground walnuts and then enough cold water to form a soft dough. Transfer the dough to a lightly floured surface, knead gently, then shape into a flat disk. Wrap in plastic wrap and chill for about 30 minutes.

Preheat the oven to 400°F.

Transfer the dough to a lightly floured surface, roll out to a disk about 12 inches in diameter and use to line the tart pan. Prick the base with a fork and chill for a further 30 minutes. Remove from the refrigerator and line the pastry dough with parchment paper and baking beans. Bake in the preheated oven for 10 minutes. Remove the paper and beans and bake for a further 5–6 minutes until the crust is crisp and lightly golden. Remove from the oven and let cool for about 10 minutes.

To make the filling, dice the Roquefort and put into a food processor. Add the ricotta, cream, eggs, walnut oil, salt, and pepper and blend briefly until mixed but not smooth. Pour into the pie crust and cook for about 20 minutes until risen and golden. Let cool slightly in the pan, then serve warm.

To make the salad, put the walnuts into a dry skillet, and toast until golden. Remove, cool, and chop coarsely. Peel, core, and slice the pears and put into a bowl. Add the arugula, parsley, and walnuts.

Put the walnut oil into a measuring cup, add the olive oil, sherry vinegar, honey, salt, and pepper, and whisk well. Pour over the salad, toss gently, then serve with the tart.

1/4 cup shelled walnuts

1/2 cup all-purpose flour

1 teaspoon salt

1/4 cup unsalted butter, diced

Roquefort filling

1/2 cup Roquefort cheese

1 cup ricotta cheese

1/2 cup heavy cream

3 eggs, lightly beaten

2 tablespoons walnut oil

salt and pepper

Arugula salad

1/2 cup shelled walnuts

2 ripe pears

8 oz. arugula

a handful of fresh flatleaf parsley

1/4 cup walnut oil

2 tablespoons olive oil

2 teaspoons sherry vinegar

1 teaspoon clear honey

salt and pepper

9-inch tart pan, buttered

baking beans

Serves 6

1²⁄3 cups all-purpose flour

1/2 package active dry yeast, 1/8 oz.

1/2 teaspoon salt

2/3 cup lukewarm water

Topping

1/4 cup extra virgin olive oil

2 large red onions, about 12 oz., cut into wedges

about 1 lb. canned sweet red bell peppers, drained

leaves from a small handful of fresh thyme or rosemary sprigs

2 tablespoons anchovy paste, or canned anchovies, chopped and mashed

16 marinated anchovy fillets

a baking sheet, oiled

Serves 4–6

To make the dough, put the flour, yeast, and salt in a bowl and mix. Add the water and mix to a satiny dough, then knead, still in the bowl, for 5 minutes or until silky. Cover the bowl with a cloth and leave for about 1 hour or until the dough has doubled in size.

Preheat the oven to 425°F.

To make the topping, heat 3 tablespoons of the oil in a skillet, add the onions, and cook, stirring over medium heat until softened and transparent. Slice half the peppers and add to the pan. Stir in most of the herbs.

Transfer the dough to the prepared baking sheet. Punch down, flatten, and roll out the dough to a circle 12 inches diameter. Snip, twist, or roll the edges. Spread all over with the anchovy paste. Add the remaining peppers, left whole, and the cooked onion mixture. Arrange the anchovies and remaining herbs in a decorative pattern on top and sprinkle with the remaining oil.

Bake in the preheated oven for about 25–30 minutes until the base is crisp and risen, the edges golden, and the filling hot and wilted. Serve in wedges, hot or cool.

A novel way of presenting this traditional Spanish dish is to cut it into uneven chunks and pile it hot and high on plates. Served with olives and glasses of chilled white wine, it makes a tasty tapas dish for a picnic. Instead of canned sweet red bell peppers, you could always use broiled or roasted fresh red bell peppers.

spanish tart
with sweet red bell peppers

leek, feta, and black olive tart
with endive and watercress salad with spiced walnuts

This tart can be made with a multitude of complementary toppings: onion, thyme, and blue cheese; wild mushroom and goat cheese; or spinach, ricotta, and pine nuts. It is quite substantial, so take advantage of the vast array of leaves now available and serve with a tasty but light salad. Slightly bitter salad leaves cut through the richness of the tart very well.

Leek tart

13 oz. puff pastry dough, thawed if frozen

1 tablespoon olive oil

14 oz. leeks, thinly sliced, about 2¼ cups

a large handful of fresh dill, coarsely chopped

8 oz. feta cheese, cut into small cubes

4 oz. pitted black olives, about ²/3 cup

sea salt

a baking pan, about 12 x 8 inches

Serves 4–6

Preheat the oven to 400°F.

Roll out the dough to fit the pan almost exactly. Trim and discard a tiny strip around the edge of the dough so that it will rise evenly.

Heat a wok or skillet, add the oil and leeks, and stir-fry. Add just a little salt, then stir in the dill. Transfer to a colander to drain. Cool.

Arrange the leeks over the dough. Top with the feta and olives. Bake in the preheated oven for 35 minutes, or until the crust has risen and is golden brown.

Serve with the endive and watercress salad (right).

Endive and watercress salad

1 cup shelled walnuts, about 4 oz.

1 tablespoon soy sauce

1 teaspoon chili oil

2 heads of Belgian endive, halved lengthwise

freshly squeezed juice of ¹/2 lime

6 oz. watercress

1 small head of radicchio, cored and shredded

1 oz. dried mango, soaked overnight, then sliced into long strips

Dressing

²/3 cup sour cream

1 tablespoon freshly squeezed lemon juice

2 teaspoons truffle oil (optional)

1 garlic clove, crushed

sea salt and freshly ground black pepper

Serves 4–6

Preheat the oven to 400°F.

Put the walnuts on a baking tray and roast in the center of the preheated oven for 15 minutes, or until golden and aromatic. Sprinkle with soy sauce and chili oil, toss well, then return to the oven for a further 10 minutes. Let cool.

Cut the endive into long strips and put in a large salad bowl. Add the lime juice and toss to prevent discoloration. Add the walnuts, watercress, radicchio, and mango strips.

Mix the dressing ingredients in a small bowl and serve separately so that the colors of the salad won't be masked by the sour cream.

Tomatoes bursting with flavor, garlic softly singing, and layers of crisp crust melting in every mouthful—what could be simpler or more delicious than this tart?

tomato upside-down tart with basil

Preheat the oven to 325°F.

Cut the tomatoes in half around the middle. Arrange cut side up in the tart pan, so that they fit tightly together. Mix the garlic and oregano with the olive oil, salt, and pepper. Spoon or brush the mixture over the cut tomatoes.

Bake in the preheated oven for about 2 hours, checking from time to time—the tomatoes should be slightly shrunk and still a brilliant red color. If too dark, they will be bitter. Let cool in the pan (if the pan is very burned, wash it out, brush it with oil, and return the tomatoes). Increase the oven temperature to 400°F.

Roll out the dough to a circle slightly bigger than the pan. Using the rolling pin to help you, lift up the dough and unroll it over the pan, letting the edges drape over the sides. Lightly press the dough down over the tomatoes, but do not trim the edges yet. Bake for 20 minutes until golden.

Let settle for 5 minutes, then trim off the overhanging edges and invert onto a plate. Sprinkle with olive oil and basil leaves and serve.

8–10 large ripe plum tomatoes (size depending on what will fit the pan)

2 garlic cloves, finely chopped

1 tablespoon dried oregano

¼ cup extra virgin olive oil, plus extra to serve

8 oz. puff pastry, thawed if frozen

sea salt and freshly ground black pepper

a good handful of fresh basil leaves, to serve

a shallow tart pan, 9 inches diameter

Serves 4

Caramelized onions smell just divine, especially when cooked in butter. These simple onion tarts, topped with creamy goat cheese, are best served warm, although they are also good cold.

onion, thyme, and goat cheese tarts

3¹/₂ tablespoons salted butter

1 lb. onions, thinly sliced

2 garlic cloves, crushed

1 tablespoon chopped fresh thyme leaves

³/₄ lb. puff pastry dough, thawed if frozen

all-purpose flour, for rolling out

8 oz. log goat cheese

sea salt and freshly ground black pepper

Makes 8

Preheat the oven to 425°F.

Put the butter into a skillet, melt over low heat, then add the onions, garlic, and thyme, and sauté gently for 20–25 minutes, until softened and golden. Let cool.

Put the dough onto a lightly floured surface and roll out to form a rectangle, 8 x 6 inches, trimming the edges. Cut the rectangle in half lengthwise and into 4 crosswise, making 8 pieces, each about 4 inches square.

Divide the onion mixture between the squares, spreading it over the top, leaving a thin border around the edges. Cut the cheese into 8 slices and arrange in the center of each square.

Transfer the squares to a large baking sheet and bake in the preheated oven for about 12–15 minutes until the dough has risen and the cheese is golden. Let cool a little, then serve warm.

Although this pie looks and tastes quite exotic, it is very simple and quick to make. The recipe calls for a jar of ready-made pesto, but if you make your own, it will be even more delicious (page 95). You can use white fish instead of salmon.

layered salmon, shrimp, and potato phyllo pie

Cook the potatoes in salted boiling water for 20–30 minutes or until tender. Drain and let cool.

Heat enough olive oil to cover the base of a large saucepan over medium heat. Add the tomatoes, garlic, and chile, reduce the heat to low, then cover and simmer for 30 minutes, stirring from time to time to ensure the sauce does not stick. Mash the tomatoes to a pulp using a potato masher. Season the salmon with salt and pepper, then add to the saucepan for 1–2 minutes to lightly cook. Transfer the sauce to a bowl and let cool. Slice the potatoes lengthwise, then put in a bowl with the pesto and toss to coat evenly.

Preheat the oven to 400°F.

Brush the base and sides of the cake pan with a little of the melted butter. Brush a sheet of phyllo pastry dough with melted butter and lay it across the pan to line the base and sides, leaving any excess hanging over the sides. Brush another sheet of phyllo pastry dough with butter and lay it at right angles to the first sheet, smoothing it down to line the base and sides of the pan. There should now be an equal overhang of phyllo all the way around the pan. Repeat with the remaining sheets of pastry dough, reserving a little of the butter.

Cover the base of the pie with half the potato mixture, followed by half the sauce and half the shrimp. Make a second layer of each and then carefully fold the overhang of pastry dough over the filling. Brush the top of the pie with the remaining melted butter.

Set the pan on a baking sheet and cook in the preheated oven for 25 minutes until golden brown.

If you are going on a picnic immediately, let cool slightly in the pan, then wrap in a clean dish towel. Otherwise, let cool completely, wrap in aluminum foil, and refrigerate until required. Serve with dressed salad greens.

1 lb. new potatoes

1 x 28-oz can chopped plum tomatoes, drained

2 garlic cloves, crushed

1 small piece of dried chile, to taste

1 lb. salmon fillet, skin removed, cut lengthwise into medium-sized chunks

1/2–3/4 cup Pesto (page 95)

6 1/2 tablespoons salted butter, melted

6 large sheets of phyllo pastry dough

6 1/2 oz. cooked peeled shrimp

sea salt and freshly ground black pepper

olive oil, for sautéing

salad greens, to serve

a springform cake pan, 9 inches diameter

Serves 6–8

6 red bell peppers, halved and seeded

1 tablespoon extra virgin olive oil

8 oz. soft goat cheese

1/2 cup mascarpone

2 tablespoons freshly squeezed lemon juice

3 tablespoons capers

2 tablespoons chopped fresh dill, plus extra to garnish

1/4 teaspoon freshly ground black pepper

slices of crusty bread, and salad greens, to serve

a 9-inch loaf pan

Serves 6–8

1 round loaf of bread, about 9 inches diameter, 4 inches high

2 tablespoons extra virgin olive oil

1/2 quantity Pesto (page 95)

2 large red onions

2 large red bell peppers

2 large zucchini

8 oz. soft goat cheese, diced

12 large fresh basil leaves

sea salt and freshly ground black pepper

Serves 6

This colorful terrine is perfect fare for a summer picnic. Make sure that it is kept cold, otherwise it will be difficult to slice.

piquant goat cheese and broiled red bell pepper terrine

Put the bell pepper halves, cut side down, on a baking sheet and place directly under a very hot broiler until blackened. Put the peppers in a bowl, cover with a lid or plastic wrap, and set aside for 10 minutes.

Line the loaf pan with plastic wrap, leaving a generous overhang. Peel off and discard the blackened skin from the peppers. Cut the peppers in half lengthwise and toss with the olive oil. Line the loaf pan with the pepper strips—depending on the height of your pan, they may not come all the way up the sides, which is fine.

In a bowl, mash the goat cheese, mascarpone, and lemon juice to a smooth consistency. Add the capers, dill, and pepper and fold through. Pile the cheese mixture into the lined pan. Fold over the peppers and then the plastic wrap and press down firmly. Refrigerate for at least 4 hours or overnight if you can.

To serve, unfold the plastic wrap and turn the terrine onto a serving plate. Peel off the plastic wrap. Sprinkle the top with a little chopped dill. Slice and serve with crusty bread and a green salad.

stuffed picnic loaf

Packed with grilled vegetables, pesto, and goat cheese, this loaf is great for a picnic. Make it a day ahead so it can be "pressed" overnight in the refrigerator, allowing the flavors to develop and mingle.

Cut the top off the loaf and carefully scoop out most of the bread, leaving just the outer shell (reserve the bread and make into crumbs for another dish). Put 1 tablespoon of the oil into a bowl, stir in the pesto, and spread half the mixture around the inside of the shell and lid. Set aside.

Cut the onions into wedges, brush with a little of the remaining tablespoon of oil, and cook on a preheated outdoor grill or on a ridged stovetop grill pan for 10 minutes on each side until very tender. Let cool.

Cook the peppers on the preheated grill or grill pan or under an overhead broiler for about 15 minutes until blackened all over. Transfer to a plastic bag and let cool. Peel away the skin, discard the seeds, and cut the flesh into quarters, reserving any juices.

Cut the zucchini lengthwise into 1-inch slices, brush with oil, and barbecue or broil as above for 2–3 minutes on each side until lightly charred and softened. Let cool.

Arrange the filling in layers inside the loaf, with the goat cheese and remaining pesto in the middle, and the basil on top. Sprinkle with any remaining oil and the pepper juices and replace the lid.

Wrap the whole loaf in plastic wrap and put onto a plate. Top with a board and a heavy food can to weigh it down. Chill in the refrigerator overnight.

To serve, cut into wedges.

roasted vegetable and ricotta loaf

This loaf looks splendid displayed whole before being sliced. The cross-section looks good too—a vision of colorful vegetables interwoven with creamy ricotta. It keeps well in the refrigerator for a couple of days.

Preheat the oven to 400°F.

Put the slices of eggplant on a baking sheet, brush with olive oil, and sprinkle with salt and pepper. Put the tray in the hottest part of the oven and roast for 20–25 minutes until the eggplant slices are tender. Put the red and yellow bell peppers and zucchini on the other baking tray, sprinkle with salt, and roast for about 20 minutes or until the peppers begin to blister and the zucchini are tender.

While all the vegetables are roasting, mix the ricotta with the lemon juice, garlic, parsley, chile, salt, and pepper.

When the eggplant slices are cooked, sprinkle with the vinegar. Put a damp cloth or plastic wrap over the bell peppers and set aside for 5–10 minutes (this makes the skins steam off and you can peel them more easily). Peel the peppers and cut each piece in half again.

Line the loaf pan with plastic wrap, then gently press slices of eggplant over the base and sides of the pan. Reserve 4 slices for the top. Spread generously with some of the ricotta mixture, then add a layer of yellow bell pepper, taking it up the sides of the pan if you can. Sprinkle with some of the basil, then spread with more ricotta mixture. Layer the red bell pepper next, followed by zucchini, adding a layer of the ricotta and basil after each vegetable. Top with the reserved eggplant slices. Cover the top with plastic wrap and put a weight on top. Leave overnight in the refrigerator.

Invert the loaf onto a plate and carefully pull away the plastic wrap. Using a serrated knife, cut into thick slices, then serve.

2 eggplants, cut lengthwise into about 5 slices

olive oil, for brushing

1 red bell pepper, halved and seeded

1 yellow bell pepper, halved and seeded

2 zucchini, sliced lengthwise

1 cup ricotta cheese, about 8 oz.

2 tablespoons freshly squeezed lemon juice

1 garlic clove, crushed

a large handful of flatleaf parsley, finely chopped

1 red chile, seeded and finely chopped

1 tablespoon balsamic vinegar

a large handful of fresh basil leaves, torn

sea salt and freshly ground black pepper

2 large baking sheets

a loaf pan, 2 lbs.

Serves 6–8

If you can find them, use the little Asian eggplants to make this dish—they look very pretty and have a more interesting texture than large eggplants.

baked eggplants with pesto

10 oz. small eggplants

¼ cup olive oil

Pesto

a large bunch of fresh basil

1 cup pan-toasted pine nuts

1 garlic clove, peeled

1 cup freshly grated Parmesan cheese

about ½ cup olive oil

sea salt and freshly ground black pepper

a baking sheet, lightly oiled

Serves 4

Preheat the oven to 375°F.

Cut the eggplants in half lengthwise and put on the baking sheet. Drizzle with a little of the oil and bake in the preheated oven for 15–20 minutes, then turn them over and cook for a further 15 minutes.

To make the pesto, put the basil, pine nuts, garlic, Parmesan, the remaining olive oil, and seasoning in a blender and purée until smooth. When the eggplants are cooked, drizzle with pesto and serve hot or cold.

Cook's tip Make twice the quantity of pesto and store the extra in the refrigerator—it always comes in handy as an easy salad dressing or tossed through pasta for a quick, delicious supper. Keep the pesto covered with a thin film of olive oil and it will stay fresh for several weeks.

Made with almonds, basil, and tomato, the pesto in this recipe comes from Trapane in Sicily, where it is known as *pesto trapanese*. It is traditionally served with a regional pasta called busiate, which is similar to bucatini. The rich smoky flavor of toasted almonds and the peppery flavor of the basil permeate the risotto rice, making the perfect combination.

risotto
with sicilian pesto

2 shallots, finely chopped

1 lb. risotto rice, preferably vialone nano

1/3 cup white wine

1 quart hot vegetable stock

extra virgin olive oil, for sautéing, plus extra to serve

Sicilian pesto

1/2 cup toasted sliced almonds*, plus extra to serve

2 large handfuls fresh basil leaves

4 garlic cloves, lightly crushed

2 x 28-oz. cans plum tomatoes drained, seeded, and chopped

1/2 cup olive oil

1 1/2 cups freshly grated pecorino cheese, plus extra to serve

sea salt and freshly ground black pepper

Serves 4

To make the pesto, put the almonds in a food processor with a pinch of salt and grind finely. Transfer to a large bowl.

Put the basil, garlic, and tomato in a food processor and reduce to a paste. Add to the ground almonds and stir in the olive oil, pecorino cheese, and a good grinding of salt and pepper to taste. Mix well and let rest for at least 2 hours.

Cover the base of a large, heavy-based pan with olive oil, heat gently, and add the shallots and 2 tablespoons of water. Cook until the shallots are transparent. Add the rice, increase the heat, and cook for 2 minutes, stirring continuously. Add the wine and let it evaporate, then reduce the heat.

Level the rice and carefully spoon 10 ladles of freshly boiled stock over the rice, cover with a lid, and cook over low heat for 15 minutes. After this time, add the pesto and mix energetically for 1 minute. Turn off the heat, cover, and let stand for 4–5 minutes.

Transfer the risotto to a serving dish or individual plates, then drizzle with olive oil and sprinkle with almond slices. Serve immediately with pecorino cheese.

* If ready-toasted sliced almonds are not available, put untoasted sliced almonds on a heavy baking sheet and bake in a preheated oven at 200°F for 40 minutes or until golden brown. Remove from the sheet and let cool before grinding.

8 baby eggplants, left whole

3–4 small zucchini, cut into 4 lengthwise

2 red bell peppers, with stalk and seeds removed, and cut into 4 lengthwise

4 garlic cloves, peeled and cut into 4 lengthwise

a thumb-size piece of fresh ginger, peeled and cut into thin sticks

6 tablespoons olive oil

sea salt

a bunch of fresh cilantro, coarsely chopped

a bunch of fresh mint, coarsely chopped

Lemon couscous

3 cups couscous

1/2 teaspoon sea salt

2 3/4 cups warm water

1–2 tablespoons olive oil

1 preserved lemon, finely chopped

1 tablespoon unsalted butter

Serves 4

This recipe is a wonderful entrée for vegetarians. For a variation, instead of roasting the vegetables, you could prepare vegetable kabobs on the grill and serve them with the couscous. Generally, eggplants, zucchini, and bell peppers are roasted together but you can vary the vegetables, according to the season.

lemon couscous
with roasted vegetables

Preheat the oven to 400°F.

Put the vegetables, garlic, and ginger in an ovenproof dish. Pour over the oil, sprinkle with salt, and cook in the preheated oven for about 40 minutes, until the vegetables are tender and nicely browned.

To make the lemon couscous, tip the couscous into an ovenproof dish. Stir the salt into the water and pour it over the couscous. Leave it to absorb the water for about 10 minutes. Using your fingers, rub the oil into the couscous grains to break up the lumps and aerate them. Toss in the preserved lemon, scatter the butter over the surface, and cover with a piece of aluminum foil or wet parchment paper. Put the dish in the oven for about 15 minutes, until the couscous has heated through.

Tip the couscous onto a serving plate in a mound. Arrange the vegetables over and around it and spoon some of the roasting oil over the top. Sprinkle with the cilantro and mint and serve immediately.

crab spaghetti
with chile mussels

This deliciously simple dish can also be made on a grill but remember to take two saucepans and a colander outside with you.

1/2 cup olive oil

1 onion, chopped

2 garlic cloves, crushed and chopped

1³/4 cups canned chopped tomatoes, 14 oz.

1 glass white wine, about ²/3 cup

1 mild red chile, seeded and finely chopped

14 oz. dried spaghetti

14 oz. cleaned fresh mussels

about 1 cup fresh crabmeat

freshly squeezed juice of 1 lemon

fresh flatleaf parsley, coarsely chopped, to serve

sea salt and freshly ground black pepper

Serves 4

Heat half the olive oil in a medium saucepan over high heat (or over hot coals, if using a grill). Add the onion and garlic and cook until softened and translucent.

Add the chopped tomatoes, white wine, chopped chile, salt, and pepper. Mix well, bring to a boil, and simmer for about 10 minutes to reduce and thicken the sauce.

Bring a large saucepan of water to a boil, add the spaghetti, and push it down into the water. Stir to separate the strands and stop them sticking together. Cook for about 9 minutes, or until al dente.

Meanwhile, discard any open mussels that will not close when tapped sharply with a knife. Add the mussels to the sauce, mix well, then cover with a lid and simmer for 4 minutes.

Drain the spaghetti into a colander. Add the remaining olive oil to the same pan, then gently stir in the crabmeat, lemon juice, and chopped parsley. Add the drained spaghetti, return to the heat, and toss well to mix all the ingredients.

Serve the spaghetti in piles with spoonfuls of chile mussels and sauce on top.

Cook's tips Try to buy a dressed crab, readily available in supermarkets, food halls, and from fish sellers by the sea. Cooking a fresh, raw crab is very simple, but extracting the meat can be a long, slow process. With a dressed crab the fiddly work is done for you, and it tastes much better than canned crab.

If any mussels remain unopened after cooking, it may be that there wasn't enough heat generated in the saucepan. Make sure the pan is boiling and covered. If any of the mussels still don't open, discard them.

stuffed greek eggplants

In Greece, these stuffed eggplants are called *papoutsakias*, which means "little shoes", and they do, in fact, look like slippers. Traditionally, the dish is flavored with basil leaves, but oregano has been used here. Don't be shocked by the amounts of garlic and oil, or by the cooking time. Serve with chunks of crusty bread and a robust red wine. Imam bayildi, the great Turkish classic dish, is similar to this recipe.

Preheat the oven to 350°F.

Using a sharp, serrated knife, cut out the central flesh of the eggplant halves, leaving a ½-inch shell. Cut the flesh into ½-inch chunks. Heat ¼ cup of the oil in a large skillet, then add the garlic and eggplant halves, cut sides down. Cook over moderate heat for 5 minutes. Remove and set the eggplant halves, cut side up, in a baking dish, ready to be filled. Leave the oil and garlic in the pan.

Put the eggplant halves in the preheated oven for 15 minutes while you prepare the filling and sauce.

Add the eggplant cubes to the oil in the skillet. Sauté for 5 minutes, then add the onion, tomatoes, celery, if using, and the dried oregano and cook over high heat. Add the remaining oil and cook, stirring constantly, until the eggplant chunks are fairly soft and the tomatoes reduced. Scoop up the eggplant pieces with some of the other vegetables, pile them inside the partially cooked shells and bake them for a further 40 minutes.

Meanwhile, add the tomato paste to the skillet, then add ¾ cup boiling water. Stir over gentle heat for a further 15 minutes to form a rich, soft, fragrant sauce, then turn off the heat. Taste and season well with salt and pepper.

After 1 hour in the oven, test the eggplants: the outer shells should be dark, wrinkled, and soft. If not, cook them for another 20 minutes. Serve the eggplants in their baking dish or a serving plate, with the sauce poured over and around. Top with the fresh herbs and cheese, if using. Serve hot, warm, or cool.

2 large eggplants, about 1¹/2 lbs., halved lengthwise

1/3 cup extra virgin olive oil

6 garlic cloves, crushed

1 red or white onion, sliced into rings

6 firm-fleshed vine-ripened tomatoes, blanched, peeled, cut into segments

2 celery ribs (optional)

1 teaspoon dried oregano

1/4 cup thick tomato paste

sprigs of fresh oregano, marjoram, or thyme (optional)

4 thin slices cheese, such as Greek kasseri, sharp cheddar, or pecorino, about 2 oz. (optional)

sea salt and freshly ground black pepper

a baking dish big enough to hold the eggplants in a single layer

Serves 4

easy fish stew

This easy, stress-free recipe makes a fantastic meal. Don't forget to provide a few empty dishes for discarded shells and some bowls of warm water for washing fingers.

1/3 cup olive oil

3 garlic cloves, chopped

2 onions, chopped

2 leeks, trimmed and sliced

3 celery ribs, sliced

1 fennel bulb, trimmed and sliced

1 tablespoon all-purpose flour

1 bay leaf

a sprig of fresh thyme

a generous pinch of saffron threads

3 x 14-oz. cans chopped tomatoes, about 6 cups

2 quarts fish stock

2 lbs. monkfish, cut into 8 pieces

1 lb. mussels in shells, scrubbed

8 scallops

8 uncooked shrimp, shell on

a bunch of fresh flatleaf parsley, chopped

sea salt and freshly ground black pepper

Serves 8

Heat the oil in a large saucepan and add the garlic, onion, leeks, celery, and fennel. Cook over low to medium heat for 10 minutes until soft. Sprinkle in the flour and stir well. Add the bay leaf, thyme, saffron, tomatoes, fish stock, and salt and pepper to taste. Bring to a boil, then simmer for 25 minutes.

Add the monkfish, mussels, scallops, and shrimp, cover with a lid, and simmer very gently for 6 minutes. Remove from the heat and set aside, with the lid on, for 4 minutes. Add the parsley and serve with plenty of warm crusty bread.

shrimp noodle broth

If you love a fiery heat, leave the seeds in the chiles.

Heat the oil in a saucepan and add the onion, ginger, garlic, and chiles. Stir well and cook for 5 minutes over low heat. Add the shrimp and cook for a further 2 minutes, then add the stock. Bring to a boil, add the noodles, and cook for a further 2 minutes. Stir the Thai basil and cilantro into the broth and serve.

1 tablespoon vegetable oil

1 onion, sliced

4 inches fresh ginger, peeled and sliced

2 garlic cloves, sliced

2 red chiles, seeded (optional) and sliced

1 1/4 lbs. uncooked jumbo shrimp, peeled

2 quarts vegetable stock

1 1/4 lbs. fresh udon noodles

a bunch of fresh Thai basil, coarsely chopped

a bunch of fresh cilantro, coarsely chopped

Serves 8

sicilian-spiced sea bass
with grilled tomatoes and baby fennel

Perfect for a barbecue, this simple dish can be cooked outdoors at the tableside. Ask your fish seller to gut and scale the sea bass for you, but if whole fish doesn't appeal, replace the sea bass with tuna or swordfish steaks.

Preheat the grill.

Crush the fennel seeds, oregano, cumin seeds, salt, peppercorns, and red pepper flakes together thoroughly using a pestle and mortar. Make 3 slashes in each side of the fish with a sharp knife. Brush olive oil all over the fish and rub the pounded spices over it and into the slits. Cut 2 of the lemons in half vertically, then cut 1½ into thin slices. Cut or tear the bay leaves into halves or thirds. Place half a slice of lemon and a piece of bay leaf in each slit. Cut each fennel bulb in quarters lengthwise and thread the cherry tomatoes onto the skewers. Brush the fish, fennel, and tomatoes with oil and barbecue over medium heat until charred, turning them halfway through, removing them as they are cooked. Serve with wedges of lemon.

Cook's tip You could cook the fish under a conventional broiler instead or, in the case of tuna and swordfish, in a nonstick skillet.

1 rounded teaspoon fennel seeds

1 rounded teaspoon dried oregano

1 teaspoon cumin seeds

1 teaspoon sea salt

1 teaspoon green or black peppercorns

¼ teaspoon dried red pepper flakes

6 small sea bass, gutted and scaled

extra virgin olive oil, to brush

3 unwaxed lemons

a few bay leaves

4 baby fennel bulbs

12 oz. cherry tomatoes

wedges of lemon, to serve

6 wooden skewers, soaked in water for 30 minutes

Serves 6

1 whole trout, about 4 lbs., filleted and skinned

12 slices prosciutto

2 tablespoons sesame oil

Cucumber salad

2 cucumbers, peeled and halved lengthwise

grated zest and freshly squeezed juice of
2 unwaxed limes

sea salt and freshly ground black pepper

an old roasting pan, lined with foil

3 oz. oak wood shavings

1 tablespoon jasmine tea leaves

a wire rack

Serves 8

tea-smoked trout
with cucumber salad

This unusual treat for the taste buds takes a little time to make, but for that special occasion it is well worth it.

Sprinkle the wood shavings and tea into the lined roasting pan and mix well. Put a wire rack that fits the pan on top.

Put both trout fillets onto a cutting board, one on top of the other, top to tail. Shape with your hands into a long sausage. Wrap the prosciutto around the fillets, overlapping slightly, to cover completely. Tie pieces of kitchen twine around the trout at 2-inch intervals to secure, then cut into 8 thick slices. Rub the cut surfaces with sesame oil and transfer to the wire rack set over the roasting pan.

Completely cover the top of the pan with foil, making sure that it is sealed all the way around the edge to stop any smoke escaping. Put the pan over high heat for 10 minutes, moving it around from time to time, to ensure even smoking.

Remove from the heat and let cool, covered, for 20 minutes.

To make the cucumber salad, scoop out the seeds from the peeled cucumber halves and discard. Finely slice the cucumber and put into a bowl. Add the lime zest and juice, and salt and pepper to taste.

Heat a ridged stovetop grill pan or a nonstick skillet until hot, add the smoked trout steaks, and cook for 3 minutes on each side. They should be brown and slightly crunchy on the outside.

Remove and discard the twine and serve the fish with the cucumber salad.

This dish can be adapted to a broiler or an outdoor grill. You would then need to sauté the tomatoes quickly in a skillet to serve with the salad.

seared tuna with tomatoes, arugula, and gremolata

To make the gremolata, grate the zest finely from the lemons, taking care not to remove too much white pith. Take the tough ends off the parsley stalks and finely chop the leaves. Roughly chop the capers, then pull all the ingredients together with the garlic on the chopping board and chop together to mix them thoroughly. Set aside in a bowl. Quarter the lemons.

When you're ready to cook, heat a ridged stovetop grill pan or skillet until almost smoking (about 3 minutes). Rub both sides of the tuna steaks with olive oil and season with salt rubbed between your fingers and black pepper. Lay as many tuna steaks as you can fit in the grill pan and cook for about 1½–2 minutes, depending on the thickness and how rare you like them. Turn them over and cook the other side for 1–1½ minutes. Set aside on a warmed serving dish and cover lightly with foil. Repeat with the remaining tuna steaks.

Rinse the pan under hot running water, dry with paper towels, and reheat until very hot. Add 2 tablespoons olive oil and tip in the tomatoes. Cook for 1–1½ minutes, shaking the pan until the skins start to split, then turn off the heat.

To serve, put a small handful of arugula on each plate, top with a few tomatoes, and lay the tuna steaks alongside. Drizzle the tuna and salad with olive oil and a good squeeze of lemon juice, and sprinkle over the gremolata. Serve with some authentic French crusty baguette or sourdough.

6 fresh tuna steaks, about 5 oz. each

12 oz. pomodorino or other cherry tomatoes

3½ oz. arugula

sea salt and freshly ground black pepper

extra virgin olive oil, to drizzle

Gremolata

2 unwaxed lemons

a large handful of fresh fresh flatleaf parsley

2 rounded tablespoons capers, rinsed if salted

3 large garlic cloves, finely chopped

Serves 6

orange and soy-glazed duck

4 duck breast fillets, about 8 oz. each

freshly squeezed juice of 1 orange

3 tablespoons dark soy sauce

2 tablespoons maple syrup

1/2 teaspoon Chinese five-spice powder

2 garlic cloves, crushed

freshly ground Szechuan peppercorns or black pepper

steamed broccoli or bok choy, or sautéed spinach, to serve

1 orange, cut into wedges, to serve

Serves 4

This is a great dish when you are short of time—it is quick to cook and tastes delicious. Serve the duck breasts with your choice of vegetables such as steamed broccoli or bok choy, or sautéed spinach.

Using a sharp knife, score the fat on each duck breast crosswise several times. Put the breasts into a shallow dish.

Put the orange juice, soy sauce, maple syrup, Chinese five-spice powder, garlic, and pepper into a small pitcher or bowl, mix well, then pour the mixture over the fillets. Cover with plastic wrap and marinate in the refrigerator for as long as possible. You can leave them overnight, but return them to room temperature for 1 hour before cooking.

Preheat the oven to 400°F.

Heat a ridged stovetop grill pan until hot, add the duck breasts, skin side down, and sear for 1–2 minutes. Transfer to a roasting pan, adding the marinade juices. Cook the duck in the preheated oven for about 10 minutes or until medium rare. Remove the duck from the oven, wrap it in foil, and keep it warm for 5 minutes.

Pour the juices from the roasting pan into a small saucepan and, using a large spoon, very carefully skim the fat off the surface. Transfer the pan to the top of the stove and bring the juices to a boil for 2 minutes, until thickened slightly. Serve the duck breasts sprinkled with the juices and accompanied by broccoli, bok choy, or spinach and wedges of orange.

chicken and tarragon pesto pasta

Pesto can be made out of most herbs, so don't hesitate to try your favorites and make your own blend for this recipe. If you like, replace the chicken with steamed vegetables such as zucchini, sugar snap peas, fava beans, or runner beans.

10 oz. dried penne pasta

1/2 cup olive oil

1 cup freshly grated Parmesan cheese

1/2 cup pan-toasted pine nuts

a large bunch of fresh tarragon, leaves stripped from the stem and chopped

grated zest and freshly squeezed juice of 1 unwaxed lemon

1 garlic clove, chopped

3 cooked chicken breasts, sliced

4 oz. arugula

sea salt and freshly ground black pepper

Serves 4

Bring a large saucepan of water to a boil. Add the pasta, stir, and cook for 8–9 minutes, until al dente. When cooked, drain and refresh the pasta in cold water, then drain thoroughly and toss in half the olive oil.

To make the pesto, put the Parmesan, pine nuts, tarragon, lemon zest and juice, garlic, and remaining oil in a bowl and purée until smooth with a stick blender.

Put the pasta, pesto, chicken, and arugula in a serving bowl, season, and toss well, coating the pasta and chicken evenly with the pesto.

Cook's tip When taking this salad on a picnic, don't add the arugula until just before eating or the oil will make it wilt.

Stuffed with aromatic, fruity couscous, this dish is really a meal on its own, accompanied by a salad.

roast chicken
stuffed with couscous, apricots, and dates

2 garlic cloves, crushed

2 teaspoons dried oregano or thyme

1–2 teaspoons paprika

2 tablespoons salted butter, softened

1 large organic chicken, about 3½ lbs.

1 sliced-off orange end

2/3 cup chicken stock

Couscous stuffing

1¼ cups couscous

½ teaspoon salt

1 cup warm water

1 tablespoon olive oil

1–2 teaspoons ground cinnamon

1 teaspoon ground coriander

½ teaspoon ground cumin

1 tablespoon clear honey

2 tablespoons golden raisins

4 oz. ready-to-eat dried apricots, thickly sliced

4 oz. ready-to-eat dates, thickly sliced or chopped

2–3 tablespoons blanched almonds, roasted

Serves 4–6

Preheat the oven to 350°F.

To make the couscous stuffing, tip the couscous into a large bowl. Stir the salt into the warm water and pour it over the couscous, stirring all the time so that the water is absorbed evenly. Let the couscous swell for about 10 minutes then, using your fingers, rub the oil into the couscous to break up the lumps and aerate it. Stir in the other stuffing ingredients. Set aside.

In a small bowl, beat the garlic, oregano, and paprika into the softened butter, then smear it all over the chicken, inside and out. Put the chicken in the base of a tagine or in an ovenproof dish and fill the cavity with as much of the couscous stuffing as you can (any leftover couscous can be heated through in the oven before serving and fluffed up with a little extra oil or butter). Seal the cavity with the slice of orange (you can squeeze the juice from the rest of the orange over the chicken). Pour the stock into the base of the tagine and roast the chicken in the oven for 1–1½ hours, basting from time to time, until the chicken is cooked.

Remove the chicken from the oven and allow it to rest for 10 minutes before carving or cutting it into pieces and strain the cooking juices into a pitcher. Heat up any remaining couscous (as described above) and serve with the chicken, the pitcher of cooking juices to pour over, and a green salad.

rosemary and lemon roasted chicken

For simple dishes such as this, quality ingredients are important. Choose an organic chicken, unwaxed lemons, a good Modena balsamic vinegar, and extra virgin olive oil.

4 lbs. chicken pieces, or 1 chicken, about 3¹/₂–4 lbs.*

3 lemons, cut into wedges

leaves from a large bunch of fresh rosemary

3 red onions

3 oz. large black olives, about 10–12, pitted

¹/₄ cup balsamic vinegar

2 tablespoons extra virgin olive oil

sea salt and freshly ground black pepper

Serves 4

Trim the chicken pieces of any excess fat and put them into a large bowl. Add the lemon and rosemary.

Cut the onions in half lengthwise, leaving the root end intact. Cut the halves into wedges and add to the chicken.

Add the olives, balsamic vinegar, olive oil, and seasoning and mix well to coat the chicken with the flavorings.

Cover and let stand at room temperature for 1 hour, or in the refrigerator overnight.

Preheat the oven to 375°F.

Put the chicken in a large roasting pan, then add the marinade ingredients. Cook in the preheated oven for 30 minutes. Turn the chicken pieces thoroughly in the pan to ensure even cooking and coloring, then cook for a further 30 minutes.

Remove the chicken from the oven. Using a slotted spoon, lift out the chicken, lemon, onions, and olives and put them on a serving dish.

Skim the cooking juices, discarding the fat. Pour the juices over the chicken and serve hot or at room temperature.

* If using a whole chicken, lay the bird on its back. Use a large knife to cut through the skin between the leg and breast of the chicken, then bend the leg backward until the joint cracks. Cut through the joint to separate the leg. Repeat on the other side.

Bend the drumsticks back away from the thighs to crack the joints, then cut through with the knife to separate. Bend back the wings of the chicken and cut through the joints near each breast to separate.

Put the bird on its side and use scissors or poultry shears to cut from the leg joint up along the backbone to the neck. Repeat along the other side. (Wrap the backbone and store for use in stock another day.)

Hold the chicken breast-side down and bend it back to crack the breastbone. Use the scissors to cut along each side of the breastbone and remove the breasts.

korean chicken

Remove any excess fat from the chicken pieces and drain off the oil while cooking.

4 lbs. chicken pieces, trimmed

1/4 cup sesame oil

1/2 cup light soy sauce

4 garlic cloves, very finely chopped

1 teaspoon chili powder

5 scallions, very finely chopped

freshly ground black pepper

1 lb. dried egg noodles, to serve

1 teaspoon black sesame seeds (optional), to serve

Serves 8

Put the chicken into an ovenproof dish, add the sesame oil, soy sauce, garlic, chili powder, scallions, and black pepper to taste. Mix well, cover, and chill overnight.

Preheat the oven to 350°F. Uncover the chicken and cook in the preheated oven for 30 minutes. Reduce to 275°F and cook for a further 40 minutes.

Meanwhile, cook the noodles according to the directions on the package. Drain, then serve the chicken and noodles, sprinkled with the black sesame seeds, if using.

chicken sauté provence-style

In the Vaucluse area of Provence, tomatoes are nicknamed *pommes d'amour*—love apples—and this dish of pan-cooked chicken, which includes lots of them, certainly inspires affection. It might once have been made outdoors, over a wood fire. If possible, try to use a youngish chicken, ideally one raised in the open, its diet enriched by corn, for the most characterful results.

Pat dry the chicken pieces and rub all over with salt and pepper. Heat the oil in a very large, heavy-based skillet or a flameproof casserole dish. Fry half the chicken over high heat for 10 minutes, pressing the pieces down hard for maximum contact with the skillet, and turning them often until golden brown. Transfer the chicken to a plate, and cook the second batch in the same way. Set aside with the first lot.

Put the onion in the skillet and sauté for 1 minute, stirring. Pour in the wine and add the bouquet garni, scraping up the sediment as the wine reduces by half. Add the tomatoes, tomato paste, and olives, and cook for 3–5 minutes over high heat, stirring. Return the chicken to the skillet, cover with foil or a lid, and cook for 8–10 minutes, or until very tender.

Mix the garlic and parsley together, then scatter this topping over the chicken and serve hot.

3¹/₂ lbs. frying chicken, cut into 10 or 12 pieces

¹/₄ cup extra virgin olive oil

1 onion, sliced

¹/₂ cup medium-dry white or rosé wine

1 fresh bouquet garni: oregano, marjoram, bay, and basil

12 oz. ripe, flavorful tomatoes, peeled and chopped

2 tablespoons tomato paste

12 pitted, salt-cured black olives, lightly crushed

4 garlic cloves, finely chopped

a small handful of fresh flatleaf parsley, finely chopped, or a mixture of fresh herbs

salt and freshly ground black pepper

Serves 4–6

These individual meat pies are a little tricky to make, but if you follow the cooking method carefully, after you have made the first one, the rest is plain sailing. They make terrific picnic food and are far better than store-bought pies.

mini pork and apple pies

8 oz. pork loin, diced

4 oz. pork belly, diced

3 slices bacon, chopped

1 oz. chicken livers

1 small onion, minced

1 tablespoon fresh chopped sage

1 small garlic clove, crushed

a pinch of ground nutmeg

1 red apple, peeled, cored, and diced

sea salt and freshly ground black pepper

Pie crust

2 1/2 cups all-purpose flour, plus a little extra

1 1/2 teaspoons salt

1/4 cup vegetable shortening

Glaze

1 egg yolk

1 tablespoon milk

6 pieces of wax paper, about 12 x 3 inches

Serves 6

Preheat the oven to 375°F.

Put the pork loin, pork belly, bacon, and chicken livers into a food processor and blend briefly to grind the meat. Transfer to a bowl and mix in the onion, sage, garlic, nutmeg, and a little salt and pepper. Set aside.

To make the pie crust, sift the flour and salt into a bowl. Put the shortening and 1/2 cup water into a saucepan and heat gently until the shortening melts and the water comes to a boil. Pour the liquid into the flour and, using a wooden spoon, gently draw the flour into the liquid to form a soft dough.

Let cool for a few minutes and, as soon as the dough is cool enough to handle, knead lightly in the bowl until smooth.

Divide the dough into 8 and roll out 6 of these on a lightly floured surface to form disks 5 inches across. Carefully invert them, one at a time, over an upturned jam jar. Wrap a piece of wax paper around the outside, then tie around the middle with kitchen twine.

Turn the whole thing over so the dough is sitting flat. Carefully work the jar up and out of the pie crust (you may need to slip a small spatula down between the dough and the jar, to loosen it).

Divide the pork filling into 6 portions and put 1 portion into each pie. Put the diced apple on top. Roll out the remaining 2 pieces of dough and cut 3 disks from each piece with a cookie cutter, the same size as the top of the pies.

Put a disk of dough on top of each pie, press the edges together to seal, then turn the edges inward and over to form a rim.

To make the glaze, put the egg yolk and milk into a bowl, beat well, then brush over the tops of the pies. Pierce each one with a fork to let the steam escape.

Transfer to a large baking sheet and cook in the preheated oven for 45–50 minutes until golden. Remove from the oven, transfer to a wire rack, let cool, and serve cold with dressed salad greens.

sage-stuffed pork tenderloin
with lentils and scallion dressing

This simple but impressive dish would suit a smart outdoor lunch. Pork tenderloin is quick and easy to cook. People seem to worry about pork being undercooked or tough, but if you follow these instructions, it will be cooked through and moist.

Preheat the oven to 350°F.

Trim the pork of any excess fat and, using a long, thin knife, pierce each tenderloin lengthwise through the middle. Push the sage leaves into the slit and, using the handle of a wooden spoon, push them further along the slit. Sprinkle the tenderloins with salt and pepper, then wrap each one in 4 slices of prosciutto. Brush a roasting pan with oil, add the wrapped tenderloins, and cook in the preheated oven for 35 minutes. Remove, let rest for 5 minutes, then cut into 1-inch slices.

Meanwhile, cook the lentils in simmering water for 20 minutes until tender, then drain. Put the scallions into a bowl, add the olive oil, wine, and sour cream, and mix. Add the bell peppers to the drained lentils and spoon onto serving plates. Top with the pork slices, scallion dressing, and chives, then serve.

2 pork tenderloins, about 14 oz. each

leaves from a large bunch of fresh sage

8 thin slices prosciutto

8 oz. brown lentils, about 1 1/2 cups

6 scallions, sliced

3 tablespoons olive oil

1 tablespoon red wine

1/2 cup sour cream

1 lb. roasted red bell peppers in a jar, drained and cut into strips

a bunch of fresh chives, chopped

sea salt and freshly ground black pepper

a large roasting pan

Serves 8

The blue cheese butter is a strongly flavored and delicious topping for the steak. A simple salad of baby spinach is the only accompaniment you'll need.

steak
with blue cheese butter

4 top loin or tenderloin steaks, 8 oz. each

sea salt and freshly ground black pepper

baby spinach salad, to serve

Blue cheese butter

4 tablespoons unsalted butter, softened

2 oz. soft blue cheese, such as Gorgonzola

1/4 cup shelled walnuts, finely ground in a blender

2 tablespoons chopped fresh parsley

sea salt and freshly ground black pepper

Serves 4

To make the blue cheese butter, put the butter, cheese, walnuts, and parsley into a bowl and beat well. Season with salt and pepper to taste. Form into a log, wrap in foil, and chill for about 30 minutes.

Preheat the grill.

Lightly season the steaks and cook on the preheated grill (or sauté in a skillet on top of the stove) for 3 minutes on each side for rare, or 4–5 minutes for medium to well done.

Cut the butter into 8 slices. Put 2 slices of butter onto each cooked steak, wrap loosely with foil, and let rest for 5 minutes.

Serve with a salad of baby spinach.

desserts

peaches in rose syrup

Voluptuous, blushy-pink peaches in a syrup of flower-scented rosé wine are a wonderfully indulgent dessert. In the South of France, where this dessert comes from, the peaches are served with *calissons d'Aix*—eye-shaped candied sweetmeats sold in lozenge-shaped boxes. Almonds, candied melon, and boiled honey syrup go into the mix, as do candied orange, mandarin, and apricot. Rice paper bases and snowy white icing complete the picture. These, with the poached peaches and rose petal decoration, create a blissful dessert. The *calissons* are hard to find outside France, so you can just serve the dessert with some delicate sweet wafers instead, if you like.

4 large, ripe peaches, ideally white-fleshed

1²/₃ cups medium-sweet rosé wine

5 tablespoons clear wildflower honey

1 teaspoon rose water

5 tablespoons *marc (eau de vie)*

16 sugared rose petals or fresh pink rose petals, to serve (optional)

Serves 4

Rub the fuzzy layer from the peach skin. Make a criss-cross cut at the stalk end and the base of each peach.

Put the wine, honey, and rose water in a deep, medium saucepan big enough to hold the peaches in a single layer. Bring this liquid to a boil.

Add the peaches and reduce the heat to a lively simmer. Splash the syrup all over the peaches as they cook, and tilt the pan to rotate them and ensure even cooking. Try to avoid stirring. Cook for 6–8 minutes minimum.

Using a slotted spoon, transfer the peaches, one by one, to a plate. Pull off and discard the skin, then let the fruit cool completely.

Let the wine syrup cool, then stir in the marc.

To serve, put each peach into a bowl. Drizzle over the syrup and scatter the petals on top (if using).

pan-grilled strawberries
with black pepper ice cream

Strawberries and black pepper are an unusual but famous food combination that works really
well. Strawberries with ice cream is also a match made in heaven, so why not combine the two ideas?
The slight heat from the pepper hits the taste buds last and marries beautifully with the sweet fruit.

1 tablespoon unsalted butter

8 oz. strawberries, left whole with green stems

confectioners' sugar, for sprinkling

Pepper ice cream

1/2 cup sugar

4 oz. mascarpone cheese

1/2 cup Greek yogurt

2 teaspoons freshly ground black pepper

an ice-cream maker or freezer-proof container

Serves 4

To make the ice cream, put the sugar and 1 cup water in a small saucepan and heat
gently until the sugar has dissolved. Let cool. Put the mascarpone, yogurt, and black
pepper in a bowl and beat well. Using a balloon whisk, beat the creamy mixture into the
cooled sweet liquid.

Transfer to an ice-cream maker and continue according to the manufacturer's instructions.
Alternatively, transfer into a rigid container and freeze for 1½–2 hours, or until the mixture
has set about 1 inch from the edge. Whisk to break down the larger crystals, then return
to the freezer for 4 hours or overnight. Remove from the freezer 15 minutes before serving
to soften.

To cook the strawberries, heat a ridged stovetop grill pan until smoking hot. Add the butter
and, when melted, add the strawberries. Press lightly onto the pan so they are branded
with black lines. Turn them over and do the same on the other side. Serve immediately, with
a dusting of confectioners' sugar and a scoop of black pepper ice cream.

Cook's tip Do not overcook the strawberries – the idea is that they remain firm with only
the outsides slightly softened by the heat.

6 tablespoons confectioners' sugar, sifted

1½ sticks unsalted butter, at room temperature

2 egg yolks

2 tablespoons ice water

1²/3 cups all-purpose flour, sifted

Lemon filling

4 eggs

³/4 cup sugar

2 tablespoons grated lemon zest and
½ cup freshly squeezed lemon juice
from 2–3 unwaxed lemons

½ cup heavy cream, plus extra to serve

*a shallow, loose-bottomed 8-inch tart pan, no
more than 1 inch deep, set on a baking sheet*

waxed paper and baking beans

Serves 4

Lemon tart—wobbly, sharp, creamy, but acidic—is an outrageously delicious dish. In France, these are often slim, very elegant offerings, not heavily filled. Ideally, make the tart a few hours before you intend to eat it, then serve it warm or cool. Some ice-cold scoops of thick, sharp crème fraîche or whipped cream are the perfect accompaniment. Serve with a small glass of citrus liqueur, dark rum, or brandy.

french lemon tart

Set aside 2 tablespoons of the confectioners' sugar and put the remainder in the bowl of an electric mixer. Add the butter and beat until creamy, soft, and white. Add the egg yolks one at a time and continue beating until well mixed. Trickle in half the ice water, then add the flour. Beat on a lower speed, adding the remaining water until the dough gathers into a soft ball. Wrap in plastic wrap, and chill for 40–60 minutes.

Preheat the oven to 350°F.

Transfer the dough to a floured work surface and roll out to ¼ inch thick. Use it to line the tart pan. Gently push the dough into the corners. Cut off the excess dough. Chill for a further 20 minutes or until very firm.

Prick the dough all over with a fork, line with waxed paper, fill with baking beans, and bake blind in the preheated oven for 15 minutes. Remove the paper and the beans. Let the dough rest for 5 minutes, then bake again for 10 minutes or until pale golden. Cut off any excess dough to make a neat edge.

Reduce the oven temperature to 250°F.

To make the filling, put the eggs, sugar, and half the lemon zest into a bowl and beat well for 2 minutes with a hand-held electric mixer. Stir in the lemon juice and cream, then pour the mixture into the tart crust. Bake for 35 minutes, or until the filling is barely set.

While the tart cooks, put the remaining lemon zest in a strainer, pour over boiling water, then refresh under cold running water. Put the zest, the reserved 2 tablespoons confectioners' sugar and ¼ cup water in a saucepan over low heat. Cook gently until the zest looks syrupy. Sprinkle the zest over the cooked tart. Serve hot or warm, with additional spoonfuls of cream.

This freshly baked, moist yet crumbly aromatic pineapple loaf needs no more than a dusting of confectioners' sugar on top. When taking a cake on a picnic, don't forget to put a knife in the tin.

pineapple and thyme loaf cake

10 tablespoons unsalted butter or margarine

3/4 cup sugar

3 eggs, beaten

1/2 cup self-rising flour

1/2 cup semolina

2 teaspoons baking powder

8-oz. can pineapple chunks, chopped in a food processor

1 tablespoon finely chopped fresh thyme

1 tablespoon vanilla sugar (page 145) or 1 teaspoon pure vanilla extract

confectioners' sugar, to dust (optional)

a 9 x 5 x 3-inch loaf pan, lined with waxed paper

Serves 8

Preheat the oven to 375°F.

Put the butter and sugar in a large mixing bowl and beat until light and fluffy. Add the eggs a little at a time, beating well after each addition; it may be necessary to add a little of the flour to prevent the mixture curdling. Fold in the remaining flour, semolina, baking powder, pineapple, thyme, and vanilla sugar.

Bake in the preheated oven for 30 minutes or until well risen and golden. When the cake is cool enough to handle, turn out onto a cooling rack and let cool. Dust with confectioners' sugar, then wrap in aluminum foil and transfer to a tin.

Wrapping fruits in foil is a great way to cook them on the grill
—all the juices are contained in the package while the fruit softens.

grilled fruit packages

Preheat the grill.

Put the fruit into a large bowl, add the orange juice, cinnamon, and sugar, and mix well. Divide the fruit mixture between 4 sheets of foil. Fold the foil over the fruit and seal the edges to make packages.

Put the yogurt, honey, and rose water into a separate bowl and mix well. Set aside.

Cook the packages over medium-hot coals for 5–6 minutes. Remove the packages from the heat, open carefully, and transfer to 4 serving bowls. Serve with the yogurt and a sprinkling of pistachio nuts.

4 peaches or nectarines, halved, pitted, and sliced

8 oz. blueberries, 1 1/2 cups

4 oz. raspberries, 3/4 cup

freshly squeezed juice of 1 orange

1 teaspoon ground cinnamon

2 tablespoons sugar

1 cup plain yogurt

1 tablespoon clear honey

1 tablespoon rose water

1 tablespoon chopped pistachio nuts

Serves 4

nectarine tart

A crumbly sweet pie crust and slivers of juicy nectarines make a sensational combination. The delicate summer flavors of white peaches and apricots are a lovely alternative filling. Come fall, don't hesitate to use plums.

Put the flour, butter, and confectioners' sugar in a food processor and blend until the mixture resembles fine bread crumbs.

Add the egg yolks and blend the mixture again, just until it comes together to form a dough ball.

Wrap the dough in plastic wrap and chill in the refrigerator for at least 30 minutes.

Knead the dough briefly to soften, then on a lightly floured work surface, roll out the dough into a large circle at least 2 inches wider than the base of the tart pan.

Drape the pastry dough over the rolling pin, lift it up carefully, and lay it over the top of the pan.

Gently press the dough into the pan, making sure there are no air pockets, then use a sharp knife to trim off the excess dough. Chill the tart shell for 15 minutes.

Preheat the oven to 375°F.

Cut the nectarines in half, twist to remove the pits, then cut the fruit into slices.

Remove the chilled tart shell from the refrigerator and, working from the outside, arrange the nectarine slices in circles on the shell, until all the fruit has been used.

Bake in the preheated oven for 30 minutes, then reduce the heat to 300°F and cook for a further 40 minutes until the fruit is tender and golden and the shell is crisp.

Dust the tart all over with confectioners' sugar, then serve hot or cold with scoops of good-quality vanilla ice cream.

Cook's tips This pastry dough is very fragile, but don't despair. Just line your tart pan as best you can, then add extra pieces of dough to patch up any cracks or holes.

Instead of serving with vanilla ice cream, you could use Greek yogurt drizzled with honey; clotted cream; sour cream, or sweetened fromage frais.

1²/₃ cups all-purpose flour

1 cup plus 2 tablespoons unsalted butter, softened and cut into small pieces

1 cup confectioners' sugar, plus extra for dusting

2–3 egg yolks

10–12 nectarines or peaches, about 3 lbs.

good-quality vanilla ice cream, to serve

a 9-inch loose-bottomed tart pan

Serves 6–8

indonesian chile fruit salad

1/2 ripe pineapple

1 ripe papaya or mango

1 pomelo or pink grapefruit

2 large bananas

2 green apples

Chile dressing

1/4 cup dark palm sugar or brown sugar

1/4 cup freshly squeezed lemon juice

2 tablespoons soy sauce

1–2 red chiles, such as serrano, seeded and finely chopped

Serves 6

To make the dressing, put the sugar, lemon juice, soy sauce, and 2 tablespoons water into a small saucepan and heat over low heat until the sugar has dissolved. Remove from the heat, add the chiles, and let cool.

Peel, core, and cut the pineapple into wedges, then chunks. Peel, seed, and dice the papaya or mango. Peel the pomelo or grapefruit, cut out the segments, and cut each segment in half. Peel and slice the bananas. Peel, core, and dice the apples.

Arrange all the fruits in a large bowl, toss gently in the dressing, then chill for about 15 minutes before serving.

summer brioche dessert

Frozen berries work just as well as fresh fruit in this delicious dessert, which means that it can be enjoyed all year round.

4 small individual brioches

1 lb. fresh or frozen and thawed summer berries

1/4 cup sugar

thick whipped cream or crème fraîche, to serve

Serves 4

Carefully trim the tops off the brioches and reserve as the lids. Using a small sharp knife, cut out a large cavity in the middle of each brioche.

Put the fruit and sugar in a saucepan and heat gently until the sugar has dissolved. Dip the brioche lids into the liquid, then start spooning the fruit into the cavity. (It looks like a lot but the brioche will soak up all the fruit and juices.) Put the lids on top at a jaunty angle and chill in the refrigerator for at least 3 hours.

Serve with cream.

This lightly sweetened and spiced cake, known as *buccellato* in its native Lucca in Italy, was traditionally made for every christening. These days, it is sometimes served as a dessert—slices are soaked in Vin Santo and covered with strawberries —but it is also delicious toasted for breakfast.

raisin and aniseed cake

3/4 oz. fresh yeast

2/3 cup milk, warmed

3 cups all-purpose flour, plus extra for dusting

1/2 cup sugar

2 eggs, beaten, plus an extra egg white to glaze

3 tablespoons Vin Santo or Marsala

3 tablespoons unsalted butter, melted

finely grated zest of 1 unwaxed lemon

1 teaspoon aniseed

1/4 cup raisins

sea salt

an 8-inch ring mold

Makes one 8-inch cake

Mix the yeast with the warm milk until dissolved then set aside. Sift the flour into a bowl and mix with the sugar and a pinch of salt. Make a well in the center and add the yeast mixture, eggs, Vin Santo, melted butter, lemon zest, and aniseed. Mix together with a round-bladed knife until the dough begins to come together. The dough should be very soft. Turn out onto a floured surface and knead for 10 minutes until smooth and elastic. Knead in the raisins. Roll into a long sausage and place in the base of the ring mold, pushing the ends together. Cover with a damp dish towel and let rise in a warm place for 1½ hours until it doubles in size.

Preheat the oven to 350°F.

Beat the egg white with a little salt until loose. Uncover the cake and brush the top with the glaze. Bake in the preheated oven for 45 minutes or until risen and deep golden brown. Let cool in the pan and when just warm, turn out and cool.

strawberry tart

When any fruit is abundant and in season, it just has to be used in a tart with sweet and crumbling crust. This combination of wild and regular strawberries is simply delicious—the tiny wild strawberries look so beautiful and are packed with flavor. If you can't find wild berries, use the same weight in regular. Any other soft fruit can be used but make sure you pile the tart high with fruit.

2 cups all-purpose flour

2 sticks butter, cut into small pieces

¾ cup brown sugar

2–3 egg yolks, beaten

¾ cup strawberry jelly, about 7 oz.

8 oz. wild strawberries

1½ lbs. regular strawberries, hulls removed

heavy cream or plain yogurt mixed with clear honey, to serve

a nonstick tart pan, 12 inches diameter

Serves 8

Put the flour into a mixing bowl and add the butter. Using your fingertips, rub the butter into the flour until it looks like bread crumbs. Add the sugar and mix. Make a well in the middle and add 2 of the egg yolks. Mix with a round-bladed knife, using cutting motions, until the mixture forms a ball, adding an extra egg yolk if needed. Dust your hands lightly with flour, bring the mixture together, and transfer to a lightly floured, cool surface.

Preheat the oven to 350°F.

Roll out the dough to just larger than the pan. Line the pan with the dough, prick all over with a fork, and chill for 20 minutes. Cook in the preheated oven for 20 minutes, then reduce the heat to 300°F and cook for a further 20 minutes. Remove from the oven and let cool, then transfer to a flat serving plate and cover with plastic wrap until needed.

Put the strawberry jelly into a small saucepan and heat gently until thin and smooth. Remove and set aside to cool a little while you pile the strawberries into the cooked pie crust, cutting any very large berries into smaller pieces. Spoon the strawberry jelly over the strawberries and serve with cream or plain yogurt mixed with honey.

Preheat the oven to 350°F.

Put the eggs, sugar, coconut, butter, ground almonds, lemon and orange zest and juice, milk, and flour into a food processor and process for 1 minute until blended. Transfer the mixture to the buttered pan and bake in the preheated oven for 45 minutes until golden brown. Remove from the oven and let cool.

Put the yogurt into a bowl and add the mint. Mix well and serve spooned over the bake.

This is simply a sublime dessert—sponge cake, coconut, ground almonds, and citrus fruits.

orange and lemon bake
with minted yogurt

4 eggs

1/2 cup sugar

1 1/4 cups dried unsweetened shredded coconut

4 tablespoons unsalted butter, softened

1 cup ground almonds

grated zest and freshly squeezed juice of 2 unwaxed lemons

grated zest and juice of 2 oranges

1/2 cup milk

1/3 cup self-rising flour

Minted yogurt

1 cup plain yogurt

a bunch of fresh mint, finely chopped

a cake pan, 8 inches diameter, buttered

Serves 8

In this recipe, palm sugar adds the most wonderful taffy flavor to the ice cream, while star anise offers a hint of something more exotic. This, combined with warm mangoes, provides a wickedly delicious dessert.

mango cheeks with spiced palm sugar ice cream

3 large mangoes

confectioners' sugar, for dusting

Spiced palm sugar ice cream

a scant 2 cups milk

1¼ cups heavy cream

⅓ cup palm sugar, grated, or soft brown sugar

4 whole star anise

5 egg yolks

Serves 4

To make the ice cream, mix the milk, cream, sugar, and star anise in a heavy saucepan and heat gently until the mixture just reaches boiling point. Set aside to infuse for 20 minutes. Put the egg yolks into a bowl and beat until pale, then stir in the infused milk. Return to the saucepan and heat gently, stirring constantly, until the mixture is thickened and coats the back of a spoon. Let cool completely, then strain.

Put the mixture into an ice-cream maker and freeze according to the manufacturer's instructions. Alternatively, pour into a freezerproof container and freeze for 1 hour until just frozen. Beat vigorously to break up the ice crystals and return to the freezer. Repeat several times until frozen. Soften in the refrigerator for 20 minutes before serving.

Preheat the grill.

Using a sharp knife, cut the cheeks off each mango and put onto a plate. Dust the cut side of each mango cheek with a little confectioners' sugar. Barbecue the cheeks for 2 minutes on each side. Cut the cheeks in half lengthwise and serve 3 wedges per person with a scoop of the ice cream.

meringues
with rose water cream

Served with rose water-flavored cream, these crispy, sugary meringues are truly sublime.

2 extra large egg whites

1/2 cup superfine sugar

3/4 cup heavy cream, to serve

1 1/2 tablespoons rose water, to serve

a small handful of clean, fresh rose petals, to decorate (optional)

2 baking sheets, lined with parchment paper

Makes 8

Preheat the oven to 250°F.

Put the egg whites in a clean, grease-free bowl and whisk until they form stiff peaks. Whisk in the sugar, one tablespoonful at a time, until the mixture is thick and glossy.

Using two spoons, shape about 16 meringues and place them on the baking sheets. Bake for about 2 hours, until crisp and dry. Let cool on the baking sheets, then carefully peel off the parchment paper.

To serve, whip the cream until it stands in soft peaks, then fold in the rose water. Sandwich the meringues together with the cream and arrange on a serving plate. Scatter the rose petals, if using, over the meringues to decorate.

seasonal fruit tarts

Once the rich but simple dough has been made, these delicious tarts are very easy. You just fill them with seasonal fruit and bake slowly. Choose from apricots, plums, apples, peaches, and nectarines. Don't worry if the dough breaks as you line the pans—just patch any holes or cracks with the trimmings. It will be topped with lovely fruit, so no one will ever know!

4 cups all-purpose flour, plus extra for dusting

5¹/₂ sticks unsalted butter, cut into cubes and softened

1³/₄ cups confectioners' sugar, plus extra for dusting

3 egg yolks

3 lbs. fruit, pitted if necessary

2 cups light cream, to serve

2 loose-bottomed tart pans, 10 inches diameter

Serves 8

To make the dough, put the flour, butter, and confectioners' sugar into a food processor and blend briefly. Add the egg yolks and blend until the mixture forms a ball. Divide in half, wrap both pieces in plastic wrap, and chill for 40 minutes.

Put one piece of dough onto a cool, lightly floured surface and gently knead to a flat disk. Roll out into a circle large enough to fit the tart pan, dusting lightly with flour to stop the dough sticking to the surface. Roll the dough around a floured rolling pin and unroll over the tart pan. Gently press the dough into the pan, pressing out any air pockets, then roll the pin over the top of the pan to remove any excess dough. Repeat with the remaining dough and tart pan, cover, and chill for 25 minutes.

Preheat the oven 350°F.

Prepare the fruit and slice, halve, or leave whole, depending on size, and arrange in the chilled, unbaked tart shells. Working from the outside in, pack in all the fruit (it will shrink while cooking). Cook in the preheated oven for 35 minutes, then reduce the heat to 300°F and cook for a further 55 minutes until the crust is golden and crisp. Remove and dust generously with confectioners' sugar. Serve hot, warm, or cold with light cream.

When freshly picked and at the height of their summery sweetness, strawberries are a joy, and they should be eaten simply on their own. At other times, they may need a little assistance to coax out their full potential. The interesting mix of flavors is an echo of the medieval, and often medicinal, use of spices and balsams.

sugared strawberries

To make the spiced sugar, put the cinnamon, peppercorns, sugar, and zest in a small spice grinder. Grind in continuous bursts to make a powdery spiced mixture.

Put the strawberries in a bowl and spoon half the mixture on top, gently stirring and mixing to encourage the juices to run. Leave for 10 minutes. Meanwhile, press the ricotta through a strainer into a bowl with the back of a spoon. Mix in the liqueur, the remaining spiced sugar, and the vinegar to form a cream.

To serve, put spoonfuls of the creamy mixture in small, stemmed glasses or glass or china dishes, then pile the berries on top and sprinkle them with a few extra drops of liqueur.

2 pints ripe, red strawberries, washed, dried, hulled, and halved

8 oz. fresh ricotta cheese, 1 cup

1 tablespoon Amaretto liqueur, plus extra to serve

1/2 teaspoon balsamic vinegar

Spiced sugar

1/2 cinnamon stick, crushed

6 peppercorns, crushed

1/3 cup sugar

3-inch strip of unwaxed lemon zest

Serves 4

traditional english apple pie

Of all the fancy desserts there are, there is nothing to beat a simple baked apple pie. It's quick and simple to make, delicious, and it lends itself perfectly to the picnic basket, hot or cold. Slivers of sharp cheddar cheese go well with it too. Children love small apple pies, which can be made in mini tart pans, but you need to stew the apple to a mush and let it cool before using.

Preheat the oven to 425°F.

Put the flour, salt, and butter into a large mixing bowl and rub in the butter with your fingertips until the mixture resembles fine bread crumbs. Add the water and work the mixture together to form a dough. This should be done quickly and lightly with your fingertips or the blade of a round-bladed knife. Alternatively, put the ingredients in a food processor and process until the ingredients are reduced to a dough.

Divide the dough in half and work each half into a neat ball. Sprinkle a clean work surface and a rolling pin with plenty of flour. Set 1 of the dough balls in the center of the flour, flatten it with the palm of your hand, and shape into a neat circle. Roll the dough one way, then give it a quarter turn and roll it the other way, shaping the dough back into a circle from time to time. Continue until the dough is slightly larger than the pie dish.

Roll the dough around the rolling pin and transfer it carefully to the pie dish, open it out, and smooth it to line the dish and the border. Fill with the apple slices, then brush the border with water. Roll out the second ball of dough as before and put this on top of the apples. Trim off the excess dough with a sharp knife. Press down the border with your thumb to seal it, creating a regular pattern around the edge as you do so. Brush the top of the pie with water and sprinkle with sugar.

Set the pie on a baking sheet in the center of the preheated oven and bake for 20 minutes, then reduce the heat to 300°F and bake for 20 minutes more. Check to see if the fruit is cooked by gently pushing a skewer into it. If it offers resistance, it is not cooked, so cook for a further 10 minutes. If you are going on a picnic immediately, allow to cool a little and wrap in a clean dish towel, and don't forget to take a pie server with you. Serve warm or cold with sugar and cream.

2¼ cups all-purpose flour

a pinch of sea salt

10 tablespoons chilled butter, diced

5 tablespoons chilled water

2¼ lbs. cooking apples, peeled, cored, and thinly sliced

½ cup sugar, plus extra to decorate and to serve

cream or plain yogurt, to serve

a shallow pie dish, about 10 inches diameter, greased

Serves 6

grilled pears
with spiced honey, walnuts, and blue cheese

A simple but delicious end to an outdoor meal—the pears, blue cheese, and walnuts perfectly complement one another. Serve on toast with a glass or two of dessert wine. For the best results, choose ripe but firm pears.

1/2 cup shelled walnut halves

2 tablespoons clear honey

1/4 teaspoon ground cardamom

4 ripe but firm pears

2 tablespoons sugar, for dusting

4 oz. blue cheese

slices of toast, to serve

dessert wine, to serve

Serves 4

Put the walnuts into a skillet, add the honey and cardamom, and cook over high heat until the honey bubbles furiously and starts to darken. Immediately pour the mixture onto a sheet of waxed paper and let cool.

Peel the nuts from the paper and set aside.

Preheat the grill. Using a sharp knife, cut the pears into quarters and remove and discard the cores. Cut the pear quarters into thick wedges. Dust lightly with sugar and cook over medium-hot coals for about 1½ minutes on each side.

Pile the pears onto slices of toast, sprinkle with the walnuts, and serve with the blue cheese and a glass of dessert wine.

strawberry and mascarpone trifle

This extraordinarily versatile dessert is perfect for a warm, lazy day. Red fruit always looks magnificent but you could also use blueberries, mangoes, and passion fruit. Only about half of the sponge is necessary for this trifle, so freeze the rest for an extra-speedy version next time round. The sponge has a dense, chewy texture to absorb the mint syrup. The mint is a perfect partner for the strawberries, but you could also use fruit juice or sweet wine.

Sponge cake

1 stick unsalted butter, softened

1 cup plus 1 tablespoon sugar

4 extra large eggs, lightly beaten

1/3 cup all-purpose flour

3 cups ground almonds

Mint syrup

3 tablespoons sugar

12 fresh mint leaves, finely chopped

Trifle filling

1 lb. mascarpone cheese

2 tablespoons sugar

3 egg yolks

8 oz. raspberries

8 oz. strawberries

a small handful of fresh mint leaves

a cake pan, 8 inches diameter, lined with parchment paper

Serves 6

Preheat the oven to 350°F.

To make the sponge cake, put the butter and sugar in a medium bowl and beat with an electric beater until the mixture is pale and creamy. Slowly add the eggs, beating well between each addition. Using a metal spoon, fold in the flour and ground almonds. Spoon into the prepared cake pan and bake in the center of the preheated oven for 40 minutes until springy to the touch or until a skewer can be removed cleanly when inserted into the middle.

To make the mint syrup, put the sugar, mint, and 1/3 cup water in a small saucepan. Bring to a boil and continue to boil until reduced by one-third.

To make the filling, put the mascarpone, sugar, and egg yolks into a bowl. Using an electric beater, beat the mixture until creamy. Using a fork, lightly mash the raspberries to a purée. Chop half the strawberries into small pieces, and cut the remainder in half, leaving the stems intact for decoration.

To assemble the trifle, break the cake into large pieces and put into a large dish or 6 individual dishes. Moisten the cake with the mint syrup and add some of the mint leaves. Spoon in the raspberry purée, then the chopped strawberries, then the mascarpone. Top with the strawberry halves, then chill in the refrigerator for at least 1 hour before serving.

Frangipane tart is one of those classic recipes that turns a seasonal summer fruit into a luxurious treat. The combination of a crisp pie crust, fluffy almond sponge cake, and tart summer fruits is a delight. Although it is not difficult to make, it does need time devoted to it, but the end result is well worth the effort.

blueberry frangipane tart

To make the dough, put the ingredients in a bowl and work them quickly and lightly into a smooth ball with your hands. Wrap in plastic wrap and chill in the refrigerator for 1 hour.

Preheat the oven to 350°F.

To make the frangipane, put the sugar and butter in a bowl and beat until light and creamy. Add the eggs a little at a time, beating well as you do so. Add the cornstarch, baking powder, and almonds, then gently fold into the mixture.

Sprinkle a clean work surface and rolling pin with plenty of flour. Set the dough in the center of the flour, then flatten it with the palm of your hand and shape it into a neat circle. Take the rolling pin and roll the dough one way, then give it a quarter turn and roll it the other way, shaping the dough back into a circle with your hands from time to time. Continue until the dough is slighty larger than the pan. Roll the dough loosely around the rolling pin and transfer it carefully to the greased pan, pressing the dough carefully into the sides. Trim any overlapping dough and prick the base with a fork.

Add the blueberries, sprinkle with the sugar, then spoon the frangipane over the top, taking care to seal the fruit completely underneath.

Bake in the preheated oven for 45 minutes or until the frangipane is well risen, golden, and springy to the touch. After 25 minutes, open the oven door carefully so as not to allow too much heat to escape and, if the tart is getting too brown, reduce the heat to 325°F for the final 20 minutes. Serve hot or cold dusted with confectioners' sugar.

1½ cups blueberries, plums, or rhubarb

2 tablespoons sugar

confectioners' sugar, to serve

Pie crust

⅔ cup plus 1 tablespoon all-purpose flour

1 tablespoon cornstarch

3 tablespoons confectioners' sugar

a pinch of salt

4 tablespoons unsalted butter, softened

1 small egg yolk

1 tablespoon dry vermouth or ice water

Frangipane

½ cup sugar

6 tablespoons unsalted butter, softened

2 eggs, lightly beaten

2 tablespoons cornstarch

2 teaspoons baking powder

⅔ cup ground almonds

a loose-bottomed tart pan or a pie dish, 9–10 inches diameter, greased

Serves 6

coconut and passion fruit shortbread bake

Dishes that are made the day before are a real bonus, especially for a picnic. With this recipe, not only is there less to do on the day but the shortbread actually improves from resting in a cool pantry. The sweetness of the coconut is balanced by the tartness of the passion fruit, creating an elegant dessert.

Preheat the oven to 350°F.

To make the dough, put the butter and sugar into a bowl and beat with an electric whisk or wooden spoon until creamy. Add the flour and rub it in with your fingertips until the mixture looks like bread crumbs. Transfer to the prepared cake pan and flatten gently with the palm of your hand and fingers, lining the base and sides of the pan. Chill while you make the filling.

Using a teaspoon, scoop the passion fruit pulp into a small bowl. Put the eggs and sugar into a large bowl and beat with an electric beater until creamy and doubled in volume. Add the shredded coconut, flour, coconut milk, and passion fruit. Using a large metal spoon, fold until evenly mixed.

Spoon the mixture into the chilled pie crust and bake in the preheated oven for 40 minutes. Remove and let cool for 10 minutes, then remove from the pan to a serving plate. Dust with confectioners' sugar and serve with a mixture of plain yogurt and cream, or with ice cream.

1 stick unsalted butter

1/2 cup sugar

1 cup all-purpose flour

Filling

7 passion fruit, halved

3 eggs

1/3 cup sugar

2/3 cup dried unsweetened shredded coconut

1/3 cup all-purpose flour

2/3 cup coconut milk

1 tablespoon confectioners' sugar, for dusting

plain yogurt and cream, or vanilla ice cream, to serve

a springform cake pan, 8 inches diameter, lightly buttered

Serves 8

An apricot tart, glazed and warm from the oven, is as welcome as the sun bursting through the clouds. This version, needing no flan tins or split-second timing, is an effortless dessert after a carefree day spent outdoors.

apricot tart

12 oz. ready-rolled puff pastry, chilled

1 egg, beaten, for glazing

1 lb. ripe apricots, halved and pitted, the pits reserved

1/2 cup apricot jam

1 tablespoon freshly squeezed lemon juice

1/4 cup vanilla sugar (page 145)

sifted confectioners' sugar, to dust (optional)

Serves 4–6

Preheat the oven to 425°F.

Unroll the dough and cut out a circle 10 inches in diameter. Re-roll the offcuts and make 4 strips about ¾ x 10 inches. Set aside.

Transfer the dough to a lightly oiled baking sheet. Leaving a ¾-inch border all round, prick the rest of the dough with a fork.

Brush the unpricked border of the dough with the beaten egg. Place the dough strips on it, cutting the ends to be joined on the diagonal and pressing them neatly together. These will puff up when baked, and act like a wall around the fruit. Brush beaten egg all over the dough, including the pricked area. Bake blind for 20 minutes, or until golden and risen at the edges. Prick once again.

Meanwhile, crack open 6 of the apricot pits. Remove and shred the kernels.

Cut each apricot half into 6 segments. Arrange them, flesh upward, on the dough. Scatter the shredded kernels over the top.

Put the jam and lemon juice in a small bowl and stir until smooth. Using a pastry brush, paint this glaze all over the fruit. Sprinkle on the vanilla sugar, then bake for 20 minutes, until the apricots are soft, fragrant, and slightly brown at the tips. Serve warm, dusted with confectioners' sugar, if liked.

Variation Red plums, nectarines, or peaches can be used in place of apricots, but do not use the kernels of plums.

This dessert works well with stone fruits too, such as plums, peaches, or nectarines.

grilled figs
with almond mascarpone cream

6 oz. mascarpone cheese

1/2 teaspoon pure vanilla extract

1 tablespoon toasted ground almonds

1 tablespoon Marsala wine

1 tablespoon clear honey

1 tablespoon sugar

1 teaspoon ground cardamom

8–10 figs, halved

Serves 4

Put the mascarpone cheese, vanilla extract, almonds, Marsala wine, and honey into a bowl and beat well. Set aside in the refrigerator until required.

Put the sugar and ground cardamom into a separate bowl and mix well, then carefully dip the cut surface of the figs into the mixture.

Preheat the grill, then cook the figs over medium-hot coals for 1–2 minutes on each side until charred and softened.

Transfer the figs to 4 serving bowls and serve with the almond mascarpone cream.

lime mousse with lemon sauce

Make this mousse the night before, as there is nothing worse than willing an unset mousse to set before serving.

1 package powdered gelatin, 1/4 oz.

3 eggs, separated

1/3 cup sugar

grated zest and freshly squeezed juice of 3 unwaxed limes

2/3 cup heavy cream

Lemon sauce

1/4 cup sugar

finely grated zest and freshly squeezed juice of 2 unwaxed lemons

Serves 8

Put 3 tablespoons hot water into a small bowl and sprinkle in the gelatin. Put the bowl into a warm oven or over a pan of simmering water, about 10 minutes. When completely dissolved, remove to room temperature and let cool a little.

Put the egg yolks and sugar into a large bowl and beat with an electric beater until frothy and creamy. Add the lime zest and juice and beat well. Add the dissolved gelatin and beat again, then set aside for 5 minutes. Whisk the cream until soft peaks form, then fold into the lime mixture. Wash the beaters well and whisk the egg whites until stiff. Add to the lime mixture and whisk briefly. Spoon into individual pots or one serving bowl. Chill for at least 2 hours, or overnight.

To make the sauce, put the sugar, lemon juice, and half the zest into a small saucepan and mix. Bring to a boil, then simmer for 1 minute. Remove from the heat and cool completely to a syrupy sauce. If it is a little too thick, stir in a small amount of water. Sprinkle the remaining lemon zest over the mousse and serve with the sauce.

lavender shortbread

Homemade shortbread is unbelievably easy to make. Cornstarch will make it smoother; ground rice or fine semolina more crumbly and rustic.

1/4 cup sugar, plus extra for sprinkling

1 stick plus 5 tablespoons unsalted butter, softened

1/4–1/2 teaspoon concentrated lavender extract or 1 tablespoon finely chopped dried lavender flowers

1 1/3 cups all-purpose flour

1/2 cup cornstarch, ground rice, or fine semolina

a shallow 11 x 7 inch baking pan

Makes 18 shortbreads

Preheat the oven to 300°C.

Put the sugar and butter in a food processor and process until light and fluffy (or beat together with an electric hand-held whisk). Add the lavender extract or flowers and whizz again. Add half the flour and pulse to incorporate, then add the remaining flour and pulse again. Add the cornstarch

and pulse again until incorporated. (Alternatively, add in stages, by hand, beating with a wooden spoon then bring the mixture together with your hands.) Tip the mixture into a baking pan and spread out until even. Mark the shortbread with a sharp knife, dividing it into 18 squares, and prick lightly with the prongs of a fork.

Bake in the preheated oven for about 40–45 minutes until pale gold in color. Sprinkle with the remaining sugar, put back in the oven, and cook for another 5 minutes. Remove the pan from the oven, set aside for 10 minutes, then cut along the lines you've marked again. Remove the shortbread squares carefully with a palate knife and lay on a wire rack to finish cooling. Store in an airtight tin.

sparkling shiraz and summer berry jellies

9 sheets of gelatin (or enough to set 1¼ pints of liquid)

1 bottle (750 ml) sparkling Shiraz or other sparkling red wine

1 lb. 5 oz. mixed fresh red berries, such as strawberries, raspberries, blackberries, blueberries, blackcurrants, or red currants

2–3 tablespoons sugar, depending on how ripe your berries are

6–8 tablespoons homemade sugar syrup* or store-bought gomme

8 shortball glasses or small glass serving dishes

Serves 8

Put the gelatin in a flat dish and sprinkle over 4 tablespoons cold water. Let soak for 3 minutes until soft. Heat the wine in a microwave or saucepan until hot but not boiling. Tip the gelatin into the wine and stir to dissolve, then set aside to cool. Rinse the berries, cut the strawberries into halves or quarters, then put them in a shallow bowl, sprinkle over the sugar, and let macerate. Check the liquid jelly for sweetness, adding sugar syrup to taste.

Put an assortment of berries in the glasses, then pour over enough jelly to cover them. Put in the refrigerator to chill. As soon as the jelly has set (about 1 hour) add the rest of the fruit and jelly. Return the jellies to the refrigerator to set for another ¾–1 hour before serving.

* To make the sugar syrup, dissolve ½ cup sugar in ½ cup water. Heat gently together in a pan. When all the grains are dissolved, bring to a boil and simmer for 2–3 minutes. Use immediately or cool and store for up to 2 weeks in the refrigerator.

sparkling nectarine and blueberry jellies

9 sheets of gelatin (or enough to set 1¼ pints of liquid)

1 bottle (750 ml) sparkling peach-flavored wine

3 ripe nectarines

2 tablespoons freshly squeezed lemon juice

7 oz. blueberries

8 rocks glasses or small glass serving dishes

Serves 8–10

Put the gelatin in a flat dish and sprinkle over 4 tablespoons cold water. Let soak for 3 minutes until soft. Heat the wine in a microwave or saucepan until hot but not boiling. Tip the gelatin into the wine and stir to dissolve, then set aside to cool. Cut the nectarines into cubes and sprinkle with the lemon juice. Put a few blueberries and cubes of nectarine in the bottom of each glass then pour over jelly to cover. Put in the refrigerator to chill. As soon as the jelly has set, add the remaining fruit and jelly. Return to the refrigerator to set for another ¾–1 hour before serving.

scented fruit jelly

Tall goblets of sweet, refreshingly cool, scented wine jelly, studded with pretty little summer fruits... what could be more perfect? Aim to make this dessert when wild strawberries or fraises de garrigue are available: their extraordinary intensity helps to make this recipe a remarkable one.

½ cup medium-dry or sweet Champagne, or sparkling white wine

6 gelatin leaves or 1½ packages (3/8 oz.) gelatin granules

3¼ cups yellow Chartreuse liqueur

6½ tablespoons Muscat de Beaumes-de-Venise

½ cup wild or small cultivated strawberries, quartered

1 cup raspberries

¾ cup red currants, half left on the sprigs to decorate, or 8 fresh cherries, plus 8 to decorate

4 x 5-oz. champagne flutes

Serves 4

Pour scant ⅓ cup of the Champagne into a heatproof measuring jug, add the gelatin, and set aside to soften and swell for 10 minutes. Mix the remaining Champagne with the Chartreuse and Muscat.

Heat the gelatin mixture over boiling water, or in a microwave on high in 20-second bursts, until the gelatin is completely dissolved. Pour in the Chartreuse mixture, stir, then cool over ice water. During the following steps, set the gelatin over the pan of boiling water now and again to keep it barely liquid.

Put a quarter of the strawberries into each champagne flute. Pour in a quarter of the gelatin mixture, then refrigerate until firm.

Repeat this layering process with each type of fruit, letting each layer set before adding the next. Place any remaining gelatin mixture over the ice water to set firmly, then chop it into tiny pieces.

Pile some of the chopped gelatin mixture onto each dessert and decorate with the reserved sprigs of red currants or the cherries. Serve cool or chilled.

pomegranate granita

This once hard-to-find fruit, a native of the Middle East, has a thick waxy skin enclosing hundreds of jewel-like ruby seeds. The juice is hailed as a great antioxidant and is now widely available in many supermarkets.

1 cup sugar

2 1/2 cups pomegranate juice

pomegranate seeds, to decorate (optional)

Makes about 2 1/2 cups, serves 4–6

In a large shallow plastic container, stir the sugar into the juice until dissolved.

Cover and freeze for 2 hours or until the mixture starts to look mushy.

Using a fork, break up the ice crystals and finely mash them. Return the granita to the freezer for another 2 hours, mashing every 30 minutes, until the ice forms fine, even crystals. After the final mashing return to the freezer for at least an hour before serving. Decorate with the fresh pomegranate seeds, if using.

orange and lemon granita

Zing zing zing! Your taste buds won't know what's hit them. Zesty doesn't even begin to describe this wide-awake, citrus assault on the senses.

1/2 cup plus 1 tablespoon sugar

6 oranges

2 unwaxed lemons

Makes about 2 1/2 cups, serves 4–6

Put the sugar and ¾ cup water into a saucepan. Pare thin strips of zest from 1 orange and 1 lemon and add them to the sugar and water. Heat gently, stirring until the sugar has completely dissolved. Bring to a boil and then remove from the heat and let cool. When cold, strain the liquid into a large shallow plastic container.

Juice the fruit and stir into the syrup to combine. Freeze for 2 hours. With a fork, mash up any crystals that have formed. Return to the freezer for another 2 hours and repeat the mashing process. Freeze again for at least 1 more hour before serving.

This would be the perfect ending to an Eastern-inspired meal. Star anise and mandarin oranges are natural partners, as both originate in China. The star anise not only adds a wonderful licorice flavor, it also looks stunning and makes for a very stylish decoration.

star anise and mandarin orange granita

¾ cup sugar

6 whole star anise

20 fresh mandarin oranges (tangerines)

Makes about 2 1/2 cups, serves 4–6

Put the sugar and ¾ cup water in a saucepan and heat gently, stirring until the sugar has completely dissolved. Add the star anise and simmer without stirring for 2 minutes. Remove from the heat and let cool.

Cut a slice off the top and bottom of each mandarin, then slice away the peel and pith. Chop the flesh roughly and process in a food processor until almost smooth. Press the resulting pulp through a strainer into a large shallow plastic container. Strain the syrup into the same container, reserving the star anise. Mix well, cover, and freeze for 2 hours or until the mixture starts to look mushy.

Using a fork, break up and finely mash the ice crystals. Return the granita to the freezer for another 2 hours, mashing every 30 minutes, until the ice forms fine, even crystals. After the final mashing return to the freezer for at least an hour before serving. Decorate with the reserved star anise, if you wish.

toasted coconut ice cream
with grilled pineapple

Toasting the unsweetened shredded coconut enriches the ice cream and gives it a lovely nutty flavor.

1 pineapple, medium or small, with leafy top if possible

1/2 cup brown sugar

1 stick unsalted butter

1/3 cup dark rum

Ice cream

1/3 cup dried unsweetened shredded coconut

1 3/4 cups heavy cream

1 1/4 cups coconut milk

1/2 cup sugar

5 egg yolks

Serves 6

To make the ice cream, put the coconut into a dry skillet and toast, stirring over medium heat for 2–3 minutes until evenly browned. Transfer to a saucepan, then add the cream, coconut milk, and sugar. Heat gently until it just reaches boiling point.

Put the egg yolks into a bowl and beat with a wooden spoon until pale. Stir in about 2 tablespoons of the hot coconut mixture, then return the mixture to the pan. Heat gently, stirring constantly until the mixture thickens enough to coat the back of the wooden spoon. Remove the pan from the heat and let cool completely.

When cold, strain the mixture and freeze in an ice-cream maker according to the manufacturer's instructions. Transfer to the freezer until required. Alternatively, pour the cold mixture into a plastic container and freeze for 5 hours, beating at hourly intervals with a balloon whisk.

Preheat the grill.

To prepare the pineapple, cut it lengthwise into wedges (including the leafy top) and remove the core sections.

Put the sugar, butter, and rum into a small saucepan and heat until the sugar dissolves. Brush a little of the mixture over the pineapple wedges, then cook them on the preheated grill or on a ridged stovetop

grill pan for 2 minutes on each side until charred and tender. Remove from the heat and, holding the flesh with a fork, cut between the skin and flesh with a sharp knife. Cut the flesh into segments to make it easier to eat, then reassemble the wedges. Serve with the ice cream and remaining rum sauce, about 2 tablespoons each.

kiwi and stem ginger sorbet

This wonderfully speckled, pale green sorbet is made using ripe kiwis and is given a lively aromatic flavor by the addition of stem ginger. For a stronger flavor, omit the stem ginger and use a teaspoon of freshly peeled and grated ginger instead.

1/2 cup plus 1 tablespoon sugar

8 ripe kiwi fruit, peeled and roughly chopped

1 egg white, lightly beaten

2 tablespoons stem ginger, drained and finely chopped

an ice-cream maker (optional)

Makes about 2 1/2 cups, serves 4–6

Place the sugar and 1 1/4 cups water in a small saucepan and heat gently until the sugar has dissolved. Bring to a boil and remove from the heat. Allow to cool and then chill.

Place the kiwi fruit in a blender and process until smooth. Add this to the chilled syrup and stir to mix well.

If using an ice-cream maker, churn the mixture until thick, add the egg white and stem ginger, and churn until firm enough to scoop. Freeze until ready to serve.

If making the sorbet by hand, pour the mixture into a shallow freezer-proof container, stir in the egg white, and allow to freeze for 3–4 hours. Place in a food processor, process until smooth, and return to the freezer, repeating this process once more. Stir in the stem ginger and freeze for 3–4 hours until firm.

You can experiment with different flavors with this delightfully elegant herby sorbet. Try Earl Grey tea with lemon balm, or jasmine tea with lemon and ginger. The wafers go well with all kinds of ice creams and sorbets.

lemon, thyme, and green tea sorbet
with pistachio and lemon wafers

3 green tea teabags

1 cup sugar

1 tablespoon fresh thyme sprigs, preferably lemon thyme

finely grated zest of 2 unwaxed lemons

freshly squeezed juice of up to 1 1/2 lemons

1 egg white, lightly beaten (optional)

Pistachio and lemon wafers

1 stick unsalted butter, softened

1/2 cup vanilla sugar*

grated zest of 1 unwaxed lemon

1 egg, beaten

1 1/2 cups all-purpose flour

2 tablespoons potato flour or cornstarch

a pinch of sea salt

2/3 cup shelled, unsalted pistachio nuts, blanched and chopped

an ice-cream maker (optional)

2 heavy baking sheets, buttered

Serves 6–8

Place the teabags in a bowl and pour over 2 cups cold water, cover, and leave overnight. The next day, dissolve the sugar in 1 cup water in a saucepan over low heat and bring to a boil. Take off the heat and pour into a heatproof bowl, then add the thyme and lemon zest. Let the syrup cool, cover, then chill in the refrigerator overnight.

The next day, strain both mixtures into a bowl or pitcher and stir in lemon juice to taste. Chill, then churn in an ice-cream maker according to the manufacturer's instructions, and then freeze. If making by hand, turn into a freezerproof container to make a shallow layer and freeze until hard around the edges. Turn into a food processor, add the egg white, and process until smooth. Repeat the freezing and beating once more, then allow to freeze firm.

To make the wafers, cream the butter and sugar until light. Beat in the lemon zest, then the egg. Sift in the flours and salt, then stir in the pistachios. Form the dough into a roll shape, approximately 2 inches in diameter, then put it in the center of a sheet of waxed paper. Roll up the paper to enclose the roll of dough, then chill until firm, at least 3 hours or overnight.

Preheat the oven to 350°F.

Using a sharp knife, cut off thin slices from the dough, 1 inch thick, and lay on the baking sheets. Bake in the preheated oven for 12–15 minutes until browned around the edges. Let cool on a wire rack.

Let the sorbet soften in the refrigerator for 15–20 minutes, then serve with a few wafers for each person. Store the remaining wafers in an airtight tin.

* To make the vanilla sugar, bury 2 or 3 vanilla beans in a jar of sugar and leave for 1 week, after which the sugar will take on the aroma of vanilla. Alternatively, for a quick version, grind 3 tablespoons sugar with a small piece of vanilla bean in a clean coffee grinder.

lemon yogurt ice cream

A light, zingy yogurt-based ice cream is lovely to serve with ripe summer berries. Make sure you choose a good-quality, creamy, whole-milk yogurt, or the ice cream will be far too acidic and the texture too icy.

2 cups plain whole-milk yogurt

grated zest and freshly squeezed juice of 2 unwaxed lemons

1/2 cup superfine sugar

an ice-cream maker

Serves 4–6

Put the yogurt, lemon zest and juice, and sugar in a bowl and stir until smooth. Churn in an ice-cream maker, then transfer to a freezer-proof container and freeze until ready to serve.

Use good, creamy, plain yogurt for this recipe and you will be rewarded with a delectable ice cream. Frozen fruit works well in this recipe too—just thaw them first. They will ooze juice, so there is no need to warm them through. The color of this ice cream is so redolent of summer that you'll be tempted to make it in the dark winter months just to transport yourself to sunnier times.

summer berry yogurt ice cream

1 lb. mixed summer berries, such as strawberries, blackberries, and raspberries

3/4 cup superfine sugar

16 oz. plain whole-milk yogurt

an ice-cream maker

Serves 4

Warm the berries and sugar in a saucepan over low heat for several minutes, until the fruit begins to release its juices. Transfer to a food processor and blend to a purée. Push the purée through a fine-meshed nylon strainer to remove the seeds. Stir in the yogurt.

Churn in an ice-cream maker until frozen. Transfer to a freezer-proof container and freeze until ready to serve.

drinks

ginger lemonade

There is something rather satisfying about being served a good homemade lemonade, particularly when you're on a summer picnic.

4 inches fresh ginger, peeled and very thinly sliced

freshly squeezed juice of 4 lemons

1 lemon, sliced

6 tablespoons sugar

crushed ice

Serves 4

Put the ginger, lemon juice, sliced lemon, and sugar in a heatproof pitcher. Add 4 cups boiling water. Mix well and let steep for 2 hours. Chill, then serve poured over crushed ice.

Variation If you don't like lemons, use limes or oranges and, for a really clean taste, add fresh mint. For something stronger, add a shot of vodka to each glass.

apple lemonade

This recipe is best made with cooking apples—they turn to delicious foam when boiled. For a quicker result, use fresh apple juice, omit the sugar, add the lemon juice, and fill with sparkling water.

2–3 cooking apples, unpeeled, chopped into small pieces

sugar, to taste

freshly squeezed juice of 1 lemon

sparkling water, to serve

Serves 4

Put the apples in a saucepan, cover with cold water, bring to a boil, and simmer until soft. Strain, pressing the pulp through the strainer with a spoon. Add sugar to taste, stir until dissolved, then let cool.

To serve, pack a pitcher with ice, half-fill the glass with the apple juice, add the lemon juice, and top with sparkling water.

homemade lemonade

You will need a juicer for this delicious lemonade—it's almost worth buying one just to make it.

¾ cup sugar

4 large juicy unwaxed lemons, plus 1 extra, sliced, to garnish

1¾ pints still or sparkling water, chilled

a few sprigs of fresh mint

a juicer

Serves 6–8

Put the sugar in a saucepan with ⅔ cup water. Heat over low heat, stirring until the sugar has completely dissolved, then bring to a boil and boil for 5 minutes without stirring. Take off the heat and let cool. Cut 2 of the lemons into small chunks and pass through the feeder tube of a juicer. They should produce about ⅔ cup thick juice. Squeeze the remaining lemons (again, that should yield about ⅔ cup) and add to the other juice. Stir in the sugar syrup you have made.

Chill the lemon concentrate until ready to use. Either pour into a large pitcher full of ice and pour in an equal amount of chilled still or sparkling water or pour a couple of shots of lemonade into a tumbler full of ice and top up with chilled sparkling water. Garnish with lemon slices and sprigs of mint.

Variation To make raspberry lemonade, purée (in a food processor or force through a nylon-mesh strainer) 1 cup of fresh or frozen raspberries and sweeten with 2 tablespoons sugar syrup (see above). Stir into the lemonade base and dilute as described. Decorate with lemon slices and a few whole raspberries.

When making iced tea, it's best to add the teabags to cold water rather than boiling water to avoid the unpleasant scum that can appear on the surface.

iced ginger tea

2-inch piece fresh ginger, peeled and finely sliced

4 black tea teabags

2 limes, sliced

lemon soda or lemonade

Serves 6

Put the sliced ginger into a large pitcher, pour over 1 quart boiling water, and let cool. Add the teabags and chill for 1 hour.

Strain the tea into a clean pitcher, add the slices of lime and ice cubes, then top up with lemon soda.

Iced lemon coffee can be just as refreshing as iced lemon tea on a hot day. It may sound a little strange, but it's very thirst-quenching.

iced lemon coffee

2 cups freshly brewed espresso coffee

sugar, to taste

1 tablespoon freshly squeezed lemon juice

lemon peel, to serve

Serves 6

Pour the coffee into a large pitcher, add sugar to taste, and stir until dissolved. Let cool, then chill until very cold.

Half-fill glasses with ice cubes. Add the lemon juice to the coffee, then pour into the glasses and serve with a twist of lemon peel.

Always make fresh juices just before serving, because they can discolor and separate quickly.

strawberry, pear, and orange frappé

1 lb. strawberries, hulled

4 pears, quartered and cored

1 1/4 cups freshly squeezed orange juice

a juicer

Serves 4

Push the strawberries and pears through a juicer and transfer to a pitcher. Add the orange juice and pour into glasses half filled with ice cubes. Serve at once.

A lovely refreshing cordial with a delicious kick of ginger—perfect for a picnic.

ginger and lime cordial

6 oz. fresh ginger

2 unwaxed limes, sliced

2 cups sugar

unwaxed lime wedges, to serve

sparkling water, to serve

1 sterilized 3-cup bottle (page 4)

Makes about 3 cups

Using a sharp knife, peel and thinly slice the ginger, then pound lightly with a rolling pin. Put into a saucepan, add the lime slices and 1 quart water, bring to a boil, partially cover with a lid, and simmer gently for 45 minutes. Remove from the heat, add the sugar, and stir until dissolved. Let cool, strain, and pour the cordial into a sterilized bottle. Seal and store until ready to use.

When ready to serve, pour a little cordial into glasses, add ice and lime wedges, and top up with sparkling water.

Almond milk is a classic North African and Middle Eastern drink. Served chilled on a hot day, it is both nourishing and refreshing. Traditionally, the "milk" is extracted from the almonds but modern recipes often add cow's milk. In Morocco, orange flower water or fresh orange rind is added to the drink to give it a floral or zesty lift and, on special occasions, rose petals are floated on the surface of each glass.

almond milk

1¹/3 cups blanched almonds

2/3 cup sugar

2¹/2 cups water

1–2 tablespoons orange flower water

rose petals, orange zest, or ground cinnamon, to serve

Serves 4

Using a pestle and mortar or an electric blender, pound the almonds with half the sugar to a smooth paste—add a splash of water if the paste gets too stiff.

Put the water and the remaining sugar in a heavy-based saucepan and bring it to a boil, stirring until the sugar has dissolved. Stir in the almond paste and simmer for 5 minutes.

Turn off the heat and stir in the orange flower water. Let the mixture cool in the pan to enable the flavors to mingle. Once cool, strain the mixture through a muslin cloth, or a fine, nylon strainer (don't use a metal one because it will taint the flavor and color of the almonds). Use your hand to squeeze all the milk out of the almonds.

Pour the cloudy liquid into a pitcher and chill in the refrigerator. When ready to serve, give it a stir and pour the milk into glasses over ice cubes, or place the glasses in the freezer so they are frosty when served. Decorate with rose petals, a fine curl of orange peel, or a pinch of ground cinnamon.

chai vanilla milk shake

The flavors of chai are wonderful combined with vanilla ice cream to make an unctuous milk shake.

1 quart whole milk

6 tablespoons light brown sugar

2 tablespoons black tea leaves

1 vanilla bean, split lengthwise

1/4 teaspoon ground cinnamon

8 cardamom pods

1/4 teaspoon ground allspice

3 scoops of vanilla ice cream

ice-cube trays

Serves 4

Put 3¼ cups of the milk, the sugar, tea leaves, vanilla bean, cinnamon, cardamom, and allspice in a saucepan and bring to a boil. Reduce the heat and simmer gently for 5 minutes, then turn off the heat, cover, and leave for 10 minutes. Strain into the ice-cube trays and freeze until solid. Freeze 4 tall glasses.

When ready to serve, pop the frozen chai cubes in a blender with the remaining milk and the ice cream and blend until smooth.

moroccan fresh mint tea

Taking a glass of fresh mint tea is an important ritual in North Africa and it is thought rude if you drink any less than two cups. The Chinese green tea used for this popular drink is Gunpowder tea, which is crisp and fresh. The tea is rolled into a small pellet, which most probably accounts for the name.

2 tablespoons Chinese Gunpowder green tea leaves or 3 green tea teabags

a handful of fresh mint leaves

6 tablespoons sugar

sugar cubes, to serve

2 heatproof glasses

kitchen thermometer (optional)

Serves 2

Put the tea leaves in a warmed teapot with two-thirds of the mint leaves and all the sugar. Heat 2½ cups water to 180°F, just before the water starts to bubble, and pour into the teapot. Let steep for 6 minutes. Put the remaining mint in 2 heatproof glasses. Strain the tea into the glasses and serve with sugar cubes, to taste.

jamaican iced ginger sorrel tea

Jamaican sorrel is the flower of a native hibiscus, sold fresh or dried in Caribbean stores or in health food shops, where it is sometimes labeled as "red hibiscus tea." In Australia and New Zealand, it's known as "rosella" and is used to make jam. It has an unusual, sophisticated taste—not unlike cranberry juice—and, if you like vaguely bitter flavors, you'll love it!

1 inch fresh ginger, peeled and sliced or grated

¼ cup dried sorrel flowers or hibiscus tea

¼ cup sugar

a twist of lime, to serve

Serves 4–8

Put the ginger, sorrel, and sugar into a French press. Pour over boiling water. When the liquid is a light purple (this happens fast!) push the plunger, then serve immediately, or cool and chill. Serve over ice with a twist of lime. To serve as a longer drink, top up with ginger ale, club soda, or sparkling water.

Variation For a sorrel rum cocktail, put ¼ cup dried sorrel, a twist of orange peel, 1 cinnamon stick, 6 cloves, and 1–2 cups sugar, according to taste, into a French press. Pour over 1½ quarts boiling water, stir well, then push the plunger. Add 2 extra cloves and a cinnamon stick to the top, cool, and chill. To serve, pour over ice, then add a jigger of rum and a cinnamon stick for swizzling.

iced peach and elderflower tea

The tea you use for this recipe should have some bitterness and tannins to contrast against the sweetness of both the elderflower and peach juice.

6 black tea teabags, such as Keemun or English Breakfast

7 cups just-boiled water

6 tablespoons elderflower cordial

1 cup peach juice

peach slices and raspberries, to serve

Serves 6–8

Put the teabags in a large heatproof pitcher or bowl and pour over the hot water. Let steep for 3–4 minutes, then remove the teabags and let cool until lukewarm. Add the elderflower cordial and peach juice and give it a good stir. Leave until cold, then add the peach slices, raspberries, and ice cubes to serve.

green tea martini

1 tablespoon sugar

1/2 cup hot green tea

2 oz. citron vodka

2 teaspoons Cointreau

an orange twist, to garnish

a cocktail shaker

2 Martini glasses

Serves 2

Put the sugar in the hot green tea and stir until it has dissolved. Let cool. Pour into a cocktail shaker with the vodka, Cointreau, and some ice cubes. Shake well and strain into 2 Martini glasses. Garnish with an orange twist.

g & tea

2 tablespoons sugar

3 tablespoons hot black tea

3 tablespoons gin

freshly squeezed juice of 1/2 lemon, plus 1 lemon wedge, to serve

3/4 cup tonic water

a highball glass

Serves 1

Put the sugar in the hot black tea and stir until it has dissolved. Let cool. Add the gin and lemon juice and stir. Fill a highball glass with some ice cubes, pour over the tea mixture, and top with the tonic water. Garnish with the lemon wedge.

blackberry tea vodka

1 quart vodka

4 blackberry tea teabags

1 1/2 cups sugar

1 lb. blackberries, plus extra to serve

ice cubes or club soda, to serve

2 sterilized 3-cup bottles or containers (page 4)

Makes 2 bottles

Put 4 oz. of the vodka in a bowl and drop in the teabags. Cover and let steep overnight. Divide the tea mixture between the sterilized bottles. Put half the remaining vodka, sugar, and blackberries in each bottle. Cover and refrigerate, shaking each day to dissolve the sugar and mix the flavors. After about a month, strain through a fine-mesh strainer, discard the berries, and rebottle. Serve on ice or with club soda, with extra blackberries.

stick drinks

Stick drinks, also known as caprioskas, are cocktails made by mashing fruits and sugar together with a stick, usually a frozen treat stick or a citrus press. You can use almost any fruit as long as you include chopped limes and sugar.

lime and mint stick drink

12 large fresh mint leaves

2 teaspoons brown sugar

1 lime, finely diced

2 large shots white rum

club soda

a cocktail shaker or pitcher

2 cocktail glasses

Serves 2

Put the mint leaves, sugar, and lime into a cocktail shaker and mash with a stick or spoon until quite pulpy.

Fill 2 cocktail glasses with ice to chill them thoroughly, then tip the ice into the mashed mint mixture. Add the rum to the mixture, shake well, then pour back into the glasses. Add a little club soda and serve.

kiwi fruit, passion fruit, and lime sticky

1 large lime, diced

1 large kiwi fruit, peeled and diced

12 fresh mint leaves

3 teaspoons sugar

1 large passion fruit, halved

2 large shots vodka

a cocktail shaker or pitcher

2 cocktail glasses

Serves 2

Put the lime and kiwi fruit into a cocktail shaker, add the mint, sugar, and passion fruit pulp and seeds. Mash well until pulpy.

Fill 2 cocktail glasses with ice to chill them thoroughly, then tip the ice into the kiwi fruit mixture. Add the vodka, shake or stir well, then pour back into the glasses.

There are so many cocktails that it is almost impossible to create a new one. This marriage with a twist of two classics, Champagne and mimosa cocktails, uses prosecco and blood red orange juice. Prosecco is a sparkling wine made in the Veneto and sold by the glass in bars and restaurants all over Venice; hence the name Bloody Venetian.

bloody venetian

2 tablespoons sugar

freshly squeezed juice of 1 lemon

1 bottle (750 ml) chilled prosecco or sparkling white wine

1/4 cup Cointreau

1/4 cup brandy

3 cups chilled blood orange juice

12 cocktail glasses

a cocktail shaker or punch bowl

Serves 12

To prepare the cocktail glasses, put the sugar on a plate and spread it out evenly. Wet the rim of a glass with lemon juice and dip it into the sugar, twisting the glass as you do so to get a good covering. Repeat with the other glasses.

When ready to serve, pour the Cointreau, brandy, and orange juice into a cocktail shaker and shake well. Alternatively, pour the ingredients into a punch bowl and stir well.

Place a few ice cubes in each of 12 glasses, then pour or ladle the cocktail carefully into the glasses, taking care not to wet the sugar crust. Divide the prosecco between the glasses and serve immediately.

This is a variation of the Cuban classic, the mojito. With the glass packed with crushed ice, this cocktail makes the perfect summer drink. Add a little extra sugar for the sweeter tooth or a little more lime for a citrus twist.

herba buena

2 oz. gold tequila

1/2 oz. freshly squeezed lime juice

1 brown rock sugar cube

5 sprigs of fresh mint, plus 1 to garnish

crushed ice

club soda, to top up

a highball glass

Serves 1

Muddle all the ingredients apart from the ice and club soda in a highball glass using a barspoon. Add the ice, muddle again, and top up with the soda. Stir gently, garnish with a mint sprig, and serve with two straws.

virginia mint julep

This recipe comes from an old American cookbook, *The Williamsburg Art of Cookery or Accomplished Gentlewoman's Companion* of 1742. This is the advice printed with it: "Two Things will inevitably ruin any Julep, the first of which is too much Sugar, and the second is too little Whiskey". Heeding the warning, the original quantity of sugar has been reduced here from 6 to 4 tablespoons. The original recipe called for whiskey made from corn, but if you can't source it, your favorite whiskey will do.

5 sprigs of fresh mint

4 tablespoons sugar

whiskey distilled from corn, such as Kentucky Straight Corn Whiskey

crushed ice

Serves 4

Divide the leaves from 1 sprig of mint between 4 tall glasses. Add 1 tablespoon of the sugar to each glass and crush together well using a swizzle stick. Add 1 tablespoon of water to each glass to dissolve. Fill the glasses with crushed ice and add as much whiskey as the ice will take. Stir well until the glasses are frosted on the outside, taking care not to wet the outside of the glass. Decorate each glass with the remaining mint sprigs and serve.

This fresh-fruit cooler always appeals due to the nature of the ingredients —there just seems to be something about raspberries in cocktails that everyone enjoys.

raspberry rickey

4 fresh raspberries

2 oz. vodka

1 oz. freshly squeezed lime juice

1 dash Chambord (raspberry liqueur)

club soda, to top up

a lime wedge, to garnish

a highball glass

Serves 1

Muddle the raspberries in the bottom of a highball glass. Fill with ice, add the remaining ingredients, and stir gently. Garnish with a lime wedge and serve with two straws.

diablo

A long refreshing cocktail with a delicate hint of black currant.

2 oz. gold tequila

1/2 oz. freshly squeezed lime juice

1/2 oz. crème de cassis

ginger ale

crushed ice

red currants, to garnish

a hurricane or highball glass

Serves 1

Build all the ingredients in a hurricane glass filled with crushed ice. Garnish with a small bunch of red currants. Serve with two straws.

old-fashioned white wine cup

The great virtue of white wine cups is that you can use a really basic, inexpensive dry white wine as the base. In fact, it's a positive advantage to do so. Most modern whites have too much up-front fruit flavor and alcohol for this delicate, quintessentially English summery drink.

1¹/2 pints very dry white wine, such as basic Vin Blanc or Muscadet, chilled

1¹/2 pints club soda, chilled

¹/3–¹/2 cup homemade sugar syrup (page 140) or shop-bought gomme

3–6 tablespoons brandy

orange, lemon, apple, kiwi, strawberry, and cucumber slices, to serve

a few fresh mint or borage leaves, to garnish

Serves 16

Mix the wine and soda in a pitcher and add sugar syrup and brandy to taste. Prepare the fruit and add to the mix, together with ice cubes, just before serving. Serve in wine glasses, garnished with the mint leaves.

This punch is very strong, so if you want to give people more than one glass, make it gentler by adding some ginger beer or sparkling water. If you can't find ginger wine, use dry sherry, then add a chunk of fresh ginger, peeled and finely sliced.

jamaican punch

freshly squeezed juice of 3 limes

1/2 bottle (375 ml) ginger wine

1 bottle (750 ml) white rum or vodka

sugar, to taste

3 limes, sliced

3 lemons, sliced

1 carambola, sliced (optional)

1 pineapple, cut lengthwise into long wedges, then crosswise into triangles

a few sprigs of fresh mint, to serve

Serves 16–20

Put the lime juice, ginger wine, rum or vodka, and sugar into a pitcher and stir until the sugar dissolves.

Fill a punch bowl with ice, add the sliced fruit, and pour over the ginger wine mixture. Stir well and serve with sprigs of mint.

A pretty spritzer to cool a hot brow during a summer picnic.

white wine spritzer

1 bottle (750 ml) white wine, chilled

4 cups sparkling water, chilled

2 cups frozen white grapes

Serves 8

Put the chilled white wine, water, and frozen grapes in a large pitcher and mix well. Serve in your favorite large glasses.

Cook's tip Frozen fruit cubes are great for chilling picnic drinks. They don't melt as quickly as ordinary ice cubes, and children love eating them too. Try chopping up orange segments, putting them in ice-cube trays, adding fresh orange juice to cover, then freezing.

americano

The Americano is a refreshing blend of bitter and sweet, topped with soda, making the perfect thirst-quencher.

1 oz. Campari

1 oz. sweet vermouth

club soda, to top up

an orange slice, to garnish

a highball glass

Serves 1

Build the ingredients over ice into a highball glass, then stir and serve with an orange slice.

Excuse the dreadful name! By adding strawberries, the rum flavor is not so strong and the drink is a little sweeter.

dark and strawmy

2 oz. dark rum

3 lime wedges

2 strawberries, sliced

ginger beer

a highball glass

Serves 1

Muddle the lime and the strawberries in a highball glass. Add ice and the remaining ingredients and stir gently. Serve with two straws.

watermelon and strawberry cooler

This is one of the easiest and most refreshing summer drinks to make, but you do really need to use a juicer.

1 large watermelon

1 lb. fresh strawberries, hulled, plus extra to garnish

1 unwaxed lemon, peeled and chopped

3 1/2 oz. vodka (optional)

3 sprigs of fresh mint, leaves roughly torn

a juicer

6–8 highball glasses

Serves 6–8

Cut the watermelon in half, then cut off a thin slice for garnishing. Scoop out the pulp and cut into rough chunks. Feed the watermelon, strawberries, and lemon chunks through the juicer alternately. Put ice cubes into a pitcher (plus the vodka, if using). Pour over the juice. Add the mint and stir well. Pour into the glasses and decorate with a slice of watermelon and a few slices of strawberry to serve.

exotic sea breeze

A variation on the classic cocktail, with pomegranate giving an exotic twist.

7 oz. vodka

14 oz. pomegranate juice

1/2 pint ruby grapefruit juice

3 1/2 oz. freshly squeezed juice from 2–3 limes

2–3 teaspoons pomegranate syrup

1 pomegranate, halved and sliced

a few sprigs of fresh mint

Serves 6–8

Pour the vodka, pomegranate juice, ruby grapefruit juice, and lime juice into a large pitcher full of ice. Sweeten to taste with pomegranate syrup. Garnish with pomegranate seeds and sprigs of mint to serve.

fruit and herb pimm's

A balmy summer's evening seems the perfect time for a glass of Pimm's, overflowing with soft fruits and fresh herbs. You can vary the fruits as you wish, but always include some slices of cucumber and a handful of fresh mint leaves.

1 bottle Pimm's No 1

8 oz. strawberries, hulled and halved

1/2 melon, seeded and chopped, or nectarine slices

1 unwaxed lemon, sliced

1/2 cucumber, sliced

a few fresh mint leaves

lemonade or ginger ale, to serve

Serves 12

Pour the Pimm's into a large pitcher and add the halved strawberries, nectarine slices, lemon slices, cucumber slices, and some mint leaves. Set aside to infuse for 30 minutes. Pour into tall glasses filled with ice cubes and top up with lemonade or ginger ale.

The refreshing lime and fresh mint flavors of this traditional Cuban cocktail mask the kick of the rum.

mojito

2 lime wedges

2 barspoons sugar

8 sprigs of fresh mint, plus 1 to garnish

2 oz. light rum

1 dash club soda

crushed ice

sugar syrup, to taste (page 140)

a highball glass

Serves 1

Muddle the lime, sugar, and mint in the bottom of a highball glass, fill with plenty of crushed ice, and add the rum. Stir well and add a dash of club soda. Add a dash or two of sugar syrup, to taste. Garnish with a mint sprig and serve.

The classic vodka and lime combination has been given a refreshing twist with a few drops of Angostura bitters.

iced long vodka

4 shots iced vodka

4 shots lime cordial

a few drops of Angostura bitters

tonic water, to serve

1 unwaxed lemon, sliced, to serve

Serves 4

Pour the vodka, lime cordial, and a little Angostura bitters into 4 tall glasses and add ice cubes and lemon slices. Top up with tonic water and serve.

sparkling sea breeze

Although the ingredients are available year-round, this refreshing sparkling cocktail works particularly well at a summer party.

7 oz. cranberry-flavored vodka, chilled

1 cup grapefruit juice, chilled (use pink grapefruit juice if your vodka is colorless)

1 bottle (750 ml) sparkling white wine or Champagne, well chilled

Serves 8–10

Pour the cranberry vodka and grapefruit juice into a large pitcher and mix well. Add the sparkling wine, stir gently, then slowly pour into the glasses.

This cocktail was named after the big artillery gun that terrorized the Germans during the First World War. A popular variation on this drink was to mix Cognac with the Champagne.

french 75

1 oz. gin

2 barspoons freshly squeezed lemon juice

1 barspoon sugar syrup (page 140)

Champagne, to top up

lemon zest, to garnish

Serves 1

Shake the gin, lemon juice, and sugar syrup over ice and strain into a champagne flute. Top with Champagne and garnish with a long strip of lemon zest.

fresh strawberry sparkler

A simple idea, but a hugely pretty one.

1 ripe medium strawberry, hulled and thinly sliced

a little sugar syrup, to taste (page 140)

rosé Champagne or other pink sparkling wine, well chilled

Serves 1

Put the sliced strawberry in the glass, add a dash of sugar syrup to taste, and top up with rosé Champagne.

fresh passion fruit fizz

This makes a romantic cocktail for two.

2 passion fruit (choose ones with slightly wrinkly skin)

2–4 teaspoons passion fruit liqueur, such as Alizé, or passion fruit syrup

cava or other inexpensive sparkling white wine, well chilled

Serves 1

Scoop the passion fruit pulp into a small strainer and press it through, scraping a knife along the bottom of the strainer to ensure you collect all of it. Spoon it into 2 chilled glasses, add the passion fruit liqueur, depending on how sweet your passion fruit is, and slowly top up with fizz.

classic bellini

The bellini was invented at Harry's Bar in Venice. It is traditionally made with white peaches and prosecco, but you could equally well use yellow peaches and Champagne.

about 1/4 cup freshly made white peach juice (from 1 large chilled peach)

prosecco or Champagne, well chilled

2 teaspoons peach-flavored liqueur, well chilled (optional)

Serves 1

Pour the peach juice to just under halfway up a champagne flute and slowly top up with chilled fizz. Stir carefully and taste, adding a little peach liqueur if you think the peach flavor needs intensifying.

Variation You can make a bellini with many different kinds of freshly juiced fruit: raspberry, strawberry, mixed strawberry and watermelon, and pear are all good. Some fruits are more intense than others—you'll need less raspberry juice, for instance, than you would peach or pear juice. Some fruits, such as peaches and pears, discolor quickly, so use them immediately or add a little lemon juice to stop them turning brown.

The ginger combines conspiratorially with the Champagne to create a cocktail that is delicate yet different.

ginger champagne

2 thin peeled fresh ginger slices

1 oz. vodka

Champagne, to top up

a cocktail shaker

Serves 1

Put the ginger in a cocktail shaker and press with a barspoon or muddler to release the flavor. Add ice and the vodka, shake, and strain into a champagne flute. Top with Champagne and serve.

It is thought that Alfred Hitchcock invented this drink some time during the 1940s in an old San Francisco eatery called Jack's. He devised it for a group of friends who were suffering from hangovers.

mimosa

1/2 glass Champagne

2 barspoons Grand Marnier

freshly squeezed orange juice, to top up

Serves 1

Pour the orange juice over the Champagne and Grand Marnier and stir gently.

Index

conversion charts

Weights and measures have been rounded up or down slightly to make measuring easier.

Volume equivalents:

American	Metric	Imperial
1 teaspoon	5 ml	
1 tablespoon	15 ml	
¼ cup	60 ml	2 fl.oz.
⅓ cup	75 ml	2½ fl.oz.
½ cup	125 ml	4 fl.oz.
⅔ cup	150 ml	5 fl.oz. (¼ pint)
¾ cup	175 ml	6 fl.oz.
1 cup	250 ml	8 fl.oz.
1 stick butter = 8 tablespoons = 125 g		

Weight equivalents:		Measurements:	
Imperial	Metric	Inches	cm
1 oz.	25 g	¼ inch	5 mm
2 oz.	50 g	½ inch	1 cm
3 oz.	75 g	¾ inch	1.5 cm
4 oz.	125 g	1 inch	2.5 cm
5 oz.	150 g	2 inches	5 cm
6 oz.	175 g	3 inches	7 cm
7 oz.	200 g	4 inches	10 cm
8 oz. (½ lb.)	250 g	5 inches	12 cm
9 oz.	275 g	6 inches	15 cm
10 oz.	300 g	7 inches	18 cm
11 oz.	325 g	8 inches	20 cm
12 oz.	375 g	9 inches	23 cm
13 oz.	400 g	10 inches	25 cm
14 oz.	425 g	11 inches	28 cm
15 oz.	475 g	12 inches	30 cm
16 oz. (1 lb.)	500 g		
2 lb.	1 kg		

Oven temperatures:

110°C	(225°F)	Gas ¼
120°C	(250°F)	Gas ½
140°C	(275°F)	Gas 1
150°C	(300°F)	Gas 2
160°C	(325°F)	Gas 3
180°C	(350°F)	Gas 4
190°C	(375°F)	Gas 5
200°C	(400°F)	Gas 6
220°C	(425°F)	Gas 7
230°C	(450°F)	Gas 8
240°C	(475°F)	Gas 9

recipe credits

GHILLIE BASAN
Almond milk
Lemon couscous with roast vegetables
Roast chicken stuffed with couscous, apricots, and dates

FIONA BECKETT
Butterflied leg of lamb with cumin, lemon, and garlic
Classic bellini
Exotic sea breeze
Fresh passion fruit fizz
Fresh strawberry sparkler
Ham and melon platter
Homemade lemonade
Kisir
Lavender shortbread
Mini pissaladières
Old-fashioned white wine cup
Seared tuna with tomatoes, arugula, and gremolata
Sicilian-spiced sea bass with grilled tomatoes and baby fennel
Sparkling nectarine and blueberry jellies
Sparkling sea breeze
Sparkling Shiraz and summer berry jellies
Sun-dried tomato, olive, and basil bread
Watermelon and strawberry cooler

SUSANNAH BLAKE
Meringues with rose water cream

MAXINE CLARK
Quiche lorraine
Raisin and aniseed cake
Sardenaira
Tomato upside-down tart

ROSS DOBSON
Figs with crispy prosciutto, blue cheese, and arugula
Mozzarella, peach, and frisée salad

CLARE FERGUSON
Apricot tart
Asparagus with prosciutto
Beggar's caviar
Camargue rice salad
Chicken sauté Provençe-style
Dried tomato purée
Fennel and orange salad
French lemon tart
Gazpacho Pedro Ximenez
Green olive and basil paste
Italian bean dip
Peaches in rose syrup
Provençal tomatoes
Red leaf salad
Salade Niçoise
Scented fruit jelly
Spanish potato omelet
Spanish tart with sweet red bell peppers
Stuffed Greek eggplants
Sugared strawberries
Tapenade

LIZ FRANKLIN
Lemon yogurt ice cream
Summer berry yogurt ice cream

TONIA GEORGE
Blackberry tea vodka
Chai vanilla milk shake
G & tea
Green tea martini
Iced peach and elderflower tea
Moroccan fresh mint tea

BRIAN GLOVER
Lemon, thyme, and green tea sorbet with pistachio and lemon wafers

JANE NORAIKA
Chilled avocado and bell pepper soup
Cilantro flatbreads with spiced eggplants and split pea dip
Eggplant and smoked cheese rolls
Grilled dill polenta with lemon, fennel, and scallions
Leek, feta, and black olive tart with endive and watercress salad and spiced walnuts
Pan-grilled strawberries
Roasted vegetable and ricotta loaf
Strawberry and mascarpone trifle
Stuffed focaccia bread
Summer brioche dessert
Tofu in a hot, sweet, and spicy infusion

ELSA PETERSEN-SCHEPELERN
Apple lemonade
Jamaican iced ginger sorrel tea
Jamaican punch

LOUISE PICKFORD
Beef tenderloin with mushrooms
Beet and pearl onion brochettes
Best-ever beef burger
Bruschetta with caramelized garlic
Charred leeks with tarator sauce
Chicken Caesar wrap
Chicken panini with roasted bell pepper and arugula aïoli
Chicken salad with radicchio and pine nuts
Dukkah-crusted tuna with preserved lemon salsa
Ember-roasted potatoes
Fava bean salad with mint and Parmesan
Fig, goat cheese, and prosciutto skewers with radicchio salad
Fruit and herb Pimm's
Garlic bread skewers
Ginger and lime cordial
Grilled artichokes with chile lime mayonnaise
Grilled duck rice paper rolls
Grilled figs with almond mascarpone cream
Grilled fruit packages
Grilled pears with spiced honey, walnuts, and blue cheese
Grilled pita salad with olive salsa and mozzarella
Grilled rosemary flatbread
Hot-smoked Creole salmon
Iced ginger tea
Iced lemon coffee
Iced long vodka
Indonesian chile fruit salad
Japanese garden salad with noodles
Kiwi fruit, passion fruit, and lime sticky
Lamb burgers with mint yogurt
Lime and mint stick drink
Mango cheeks with spiced palm sugar ice cream
Mini pork and apple pies
Mixed mushroom frittata
Moroccan fish skewers with couscous
Mushroom burgers with onion jam
Onion, thyme, and goat cheese tarts
Orange and soy-glazed duck
Orzo salad with lemon and herb dressing
Oysters with spicy chorizo
Pasta, squash, and feta salad with olive dressing
Pepper 'n' spice chicken
Peppered tuna steak with salsa rossa
Red snapper with parsley salad
Roquefort and walnut tart
Shrimp and beef satays
Shrimp, chorizo, and sage skewers
Smoky spareribs
Souvlaki with cracked wheat salad
Squid piri-piri
Steak with blue cheese butter
Strawberry, pear, and orange frappé
Stuffed picnic loaf
Summer vegetables with bagna cauda
Thai-style beef salad
Three salsas
Toasted coconut ice cream with grilled pineapple
Vietnamese pork balls
Whole chicken roasted on the grill
Whole salmon stuffed with herbs
Zucchini, feta, and mint salad

BEN REED
Americano
Dark and strawmy
Diablo
French 75
Ginger champagne
Herba Buena
Mimosa
Mojito
Raspberry rickey

FIONA SMITH
Piquant goat cheese and broiled red bell pepper terrine

SUNIL VIJAYAKAR
Kiwi and stem ginger sorbet
Orange and lemon granita
Pomegranate granita
Star anise and mandarin granita

FRAN WARDE
Baked eggplant with pesto sauce
Bean and mint salad
Chicken and tarragon pesto pasta
Coconut and passion fruit shortbread bake
Crab spaghetti with chile mussels
Easy fish stew
Ginger lemonade
Grilled zucchini
Korean chicken

Leaf and herb salad
Lime mousse with lemon sauce
Lobster salad with chile dressing
Nectarine tart
Orange and lemon bake with minted yogurt
Rosemary and lemon roasted chicken
Sage-stuffed pork tenderloin with lentils and scallion dressing
Seasonal fruit tarts
Sesame-crusted marlin with ginger dressing
Shrimp noodle broth
Strawberry tart
Summer salad
Sweet glazed bell pepper salad
Swordfish with salsa
Tea-smoked trout with cucumber salad
Toasted ciabatta pizzas
Turkish toasted bread
Turmeric lamb with couscous salad
White wine spritzer

LINDY WILDSMITH
Aromatic pork burger in pita bread
Bloody Venetian
Blueberry frangipane tart
Chilled spinach, arugula, and watercress soup
Hot crusty loaf filled with mozzarella, salami, and tomato
Layered salmon, shrimp, and potato phyllo pie
Pineapple and thyme loaf cake
Risotto with Sicilian pesto
Traditional English apple pie
Virginia mint julep

---

photography credits

JAN BALDWIN
Pages 4 (Camp Kent designed by Alexandra Champalimaud www.alexchamp.com), 10l, 24l (Suzy & Graham Hursts' house in Palm Beach, Sydney, New South Wales), 30b, 91b, 127l (designed by Stephen Blatt Architects www.sbarchitects.com), 149ar, 149bc (www.alexchamp.com as before), 155l (interior designer Philip Hooper's home in East Sussex) 157l (Laurence & Yves Sabourets' house in Brittany), 166l

MARTIN BRIGDALE
Pages 8, 17l, 27, 28, 30ar, 31, 35, 38a, 46a, 79r, 82, 84, 87, 89a, 91a, 96, 99, 115al, 118 both, 119, 128, 130, 131 all, 134l, 155r, 157r, 158l, 160, 161

PETER CASSIDY
Pages 9ar, 11, 13a, 14a, 15, 22, 32, 39r, 41a, 41br, 46b both, 74, 92, 97 both, 102 both, 103, 104 both, 107, 110, 114, 115ac, 116, 124, 126l, 137, 138r, 139, 140 both, 141 all, 149bl, 151, 154, 163r, 167r, 172l

CHRISTOPHER DRAKE
Page 90a (Maurizio Epifani, owner of L'oro dei Farlocchi/www.lorodeifarlocchi.com)

STYLED BY ENRICA STABILE:
Pages 1-3, 6, 29l, 38b (Siegliende Wondert's terrace in Milan) 39l, 51ac, 53a (a Soho roof top New York), 57r (garden designer Mary Z. Jenkins's house in New York), 89b, 101 inset, 106l Enrica Stabile, antiques dealer, interior decorator and photographic stylist:
L'Utile e il Dilettevole (shop)
Via Carlo Maria Maggi 6
20154 Milano
+39 0234 53 60 86
www.enricastabile.com

RICHARD JUNG
Pages 42a, 49l, 85, 142 both, 144, 145 both

WILLIAM LINGWOOD
Pages 21, 24r, 30al, 53b, 54r, 55, 88l, 94, 117, 122, 133, 146a, 147r, 156 both, 162, 163l, 164r, 166r, 169, 170r, 173

PAUL MASSEY
Pages 17r, 18l, 20a (the home in Denmark of Charlotte Lynggaard, designer of Ole Lynggaard Copenhagen/www.olelynggaard.dk), 41bl, 76l, 79l (Hôtel Le Sénéchal, Ars en Ré, designed by Christophe Ducharme Architecte/ www.hotel-le-senechal.co.uk), 134r, 147l, 152r (the Barton's seaside home in West Sussex: www.thedodo.co.uk), 159r, 167l

JAMES MERRELL
Page 164l

CLAIRE RICHARDSON
Page 172r

DEBI TRELOAR
Pages 5, 9ac, 14b, 23, 33al, 33ac, 34 both, 37 both, 44b, 45l, 48 both, 51al, 52a, 63 both, 64 both, 77l, 83ar, 88r, 95 all, 98all, 100, 101 main, 106r, 108, 109 both, 113, 115ar, 120l (Riad Chambres d'Amis in Marrakech (B&B), designed and owned by Ank de la Plume, decorated in co-production with Household Hardware and Rutger Jan de Lange: www.chambresdamis.com), 121, 125 all, 126r, 129 both, 135 both, 138l, 146b (www.chambresdamis.com as before), 148, 149al, 150, 165, 170l

CHRIS TUBBS
Endpapers, pages 83al (Vanni & Nicoletta Calamai's home near Siena), 83c (Toia Saibene & Giuliana Magnifico's home in Lucignano, Tuscany), 83b (designer Gabriella Cantaluppi Abbado's home in Monticchiello +39 333 90 30 809), 86a (Toia Saibene & Giuliana Magnifico's home in Lucignano, Tuscany)

IAN WALLACE
Pages 9al, 9b, 10r, 13b, 16, 18r, 19, 20b, 25 both, 26, 29r, 33ar, 33b, 36, 42b, 43, 44a, 45r, 47, 49r, 50, 51ar, 51b, 52b, 54l, 56 both, 57l, 58, 59 both, 60, 61, 62, 65, 66, 67 both, 68, 69, 70, 71 all, 72, 73, 75, 76r, 77r, 78 both, 80 both, 81, 86b, 90b, 93, 105, 111 both, 112, 115b, 120r, 123, 127r, 132, 136, 143, 149br, 152l, 153, 158-159, 168 both, 171